Gëzim Hajdari

Selected Poems

ALSO BY GËZIM HAJDARI IN ENGLISH TRANSLATION

Stigmata (translated by Cristina Viti)
Bitter Grass (translated by Ian Seed)

Gëzim Hajdari

Selected Poems
(1990–2020)

*Translated from Italian
by Sarah Stickney*

Shearsman Books

First published in the United Kingdom in 2025 by
Shearsman Books Ltd
P.O. Box 4239
Swindon
SN3 9FN

Shearsman Books Ltd Registered Office
30-31 St James Place, Mangotsfield, Bristol BS16 9JB
(this address not for correspondence)

www.shearsman.com

EU AUTHORISED REPRESENTATIVE:
Lightning Source France
1 Av. Johannes Gutenberg, 78310 Maurepas, France
Email: compliance@lightningsource.fr

ISBN 978-1-84861-961-6

This selection copyright © Gëzim Hajdari 2025
Translations © Sarah Stickney 2025

The right of Gëzim Hajdari to be identified as the author of this work, and of Sarah Stickney to be identified as the translator thereof, has been asserted by them in accordance with Section 77 of the Copyright, Designs and Patents Act 1988.

All rights reserved

This book is copyright. Subject to statutory exception and to provisions of relevant collective licensing agreements, no reproduction of any part may take place without the prior written permission of Shearsman Books Ltd.

The work presented in this volume is taken from the author's *Poesie scelte* (Nardò, Italy: Besa Muci Editore, 2021)

CONTENTS

Translator's introduction / 11
'Salt and Heart: On the translation of Hajdari's Poetry'

from BITTER GRASS (1976 / 2001 / 2013)

No one knows if I'm still hanging on / 16
They'll find me in the harvested fields / 17
Even from beyond the grave / 18
Hanging from a nail / 19
Tormented now I wander the country / 20
Nothing dawns / 21
Immense like you, hill / 22
We'll walk the dew-white morning / 23
Often in the depths of night / 24
No one can ever know / 25
I don't care / 25
Moon / 26
Don't despair / 26
Don't cry / 27
Chasing the cuckoo / 27
At the bottom of the garden / 28
My country / 28
This evening I want someone to call me / 29

from RAIN ANTHOLOGY (1990 / 2000)

I now believe in nothing! / 31
Here in rain's homeland / 32
Maybe the barren hills of Darsìa / 32
Is it true that in your heart / 33
I'm witness to your ancient cry / 34
Stony, closed skies / 34
Beside me nothing flows / 35
Nights as black as dogs' eyes / 35

At the top of the hill / 36
Stepmother land / 36
If Spring beats you to Kupas / 37
All of your tragedy, History / 38

from DOG SHADOW (1993)

A blind verse / 39
Mother / 39
What am I waiting for in this empty room? / 39
It rains constantly / 39
Ever more alone here in the West / 40
Where's your holiness Rome / 40
How sad they are / 40

from STONES WINDWARD (1995)

Will there be other possibilities? / 41
Who's that singing in the fog? / 41
We smell the smell of blood / 41
This closed sky / 42
Nothing remains of those dreams / 42
We get lost in the mist / 42
Forgetting we are blind / 43
No other gesture is possible / 43

from BODY PRESENT (1999)

I sing my body present / 44
I'm a bell of the sea / 45
By now this country's language / 46
Those who continue to flee in the snow / 47
We are here among stones / 48
We cling to our names / 49

We can't find a way to speak / 49
September is the month / 50
What exists outside / 51
In the valley / 51
I'll remain / 52
How sad Rome is / 53
You live facing winter / 54
I'm the truth / 55
You tell me that yesterday / 56
The weightless extension of fields / 57
I fold into nothing / 58
We take refuge in our light bodies / 59
Wherever I go in the West / 59

from STIGMATA (2002)

I'm leaving these lines like a goodbye / 60
This evening I'm waiting for the border-snow / 61
I listen to my silence / 62
How poor we are / 62
River, you must tell how I was also here / 63
That's my skin hanging from the wind and ringing / 63
Every day I create a new homeland / 64
In which season do I seek you / 64
Returning to Ciociaria in full May / 65
When you disembarked in the port of Trieste / 66
For you men of Europe / 67
I often dream of returning to the hills / 68
My body shakes / 69
I am a man of the border / 70

from BLACK THORNS (2004)

You all came here to live next to me in the West / 71
One day we will also become Darsìa / 72

The hill of Judas Trees / 72
I want my body to rest far from the homeland / 73
Don't forget the river / 73
You announce springtime / 73
Black thorns / 74
Western world, where is your *besa*? / 77

from MOONACHE (2005)

The stillness of your body without masks / 80
To come back to the border I had to cross my wound / 80
Take me to my homeland / 81
I told you my best book / 81
I've waited a long time for this day / 82
For years I've lunched in Frosinone's Mirabar / 82
How wonderful it is to hear your words / 83
We've waited so long to speak / 84
Ever since the rainy season arrived / 85
I don't know why I thought of you / 5
Wild Rose / 86
Moonache / 89

from PELIGÒRGA (2007)

I don't know what awaits me / 94
My mother came from the city / 95
When I grew up my parents wanted me / 96
Where are you fleeing my childhood / 98
How I suffered / 99
I had just turned ten / 100
Perhaps one day my trembling body / 102
My father was sixteen years old / 103
I celebrated ferragosto / 106
Balkan spring / 106
I want the pages of my books / 106
Tending your vines / 107

from DELTA OF YOUR RIVER (2015)

I am going away Europe / 114
You're a black goddess / 116
I danced with the Masai / 117
Your naked skin / 118
Vast evenings of flame / 118
Where do these bloody men go / 119
All the way out here in Ciociaria / 119
The blind night on the walls of Arusha / 120
I crossed the Sahara / 120
On the dusty streets of Bamako / 121
The women of Segou do their washing / 121
The young cheleb with their muscled / 122
I arrived at Cairo by night / 123
Equatorial night / 123
Vultures and black clouds in the sky / 124
It's big, Uganda's moon / 124
Keeper of my grapevine / 125
Delta of your river / 130

from INSIDE ME GROWS A FOREIGN MAN (2020)

I am a poet banished to the heart of Europe / 134
Why did you cause me to be born Albanian / 135
My twenty-seventh year in exile / 136
People see me walking the streets of Ciociaria / 138
The wife of my Albanian friend Tefik / 139
You, my dear old mother, you have closed / 140
His menacing voice every morning early / 142
Nails of exile / 144
I gather the forgotten fruit that hangs on the trees by the road / 148
You don't know the wounds of the south / 149
Running against the wind towards the mountain / 151
Rise Jesus, take up your lash / 152
Marsala / 160

Catania / 161
Elegy for my friends the exiled poets / 162
At dawn naked, untraversed streets surround me / 176
I turn to you, weak and partial men / 177
My poetry: a sovereign country / 178
They flee towards the North, the West / 178
Kamal's lament / 179
March 21st the bats fly over the hills of Ciociaria / 182
The sound of bagpipes moves out / 183
To live in bitter enemy lands suspended / 185
Where do they lead us, these voices we hear… / 186
It's snowing on Dartmoor / 187
Waiting for the call / 188
The bitter bread of barbarians / 189
Infinite rains falling through the years / 191
Remaining without a home / 192

TRANSLATOR'S INTRODUCTION

Salt and Heart[1]:
On the translation of Hajdari's Poetry

I initially encountered the poetry of Gëzim Hajdari through Professor Graziella Parati, one of the first scholars I met working in the field of the *Scrittori Migranti* or "Migrant Writers" as these translingual writers were then called. I was drawn to the linguistic and emotional breadth that writing in a second language necessitates, and interested in the complex internal dialogue that such work involves. I was still in graduate school and just starting out as a translator when Professor Parati kindly put me in touch with Hajdari. The poet responded with great kindness and enthusiasm to the tentative letter I wrote him in which I asked if he might take me on as the translator of his work.

Looking back, that generous literary welcome epitomizes Hajdari's life and work. The antagonism that his own country has demonstrated towards him and his work has only encouraged him in his literary hospitality. As writers and scholars have noted, his poetry contains a decolonizing force within its language, and Hajdari's egalitarian and welcoming stance in life mirrors that of his work. Our connection and my interest in his work earned me a Fulbright Grant to translate his poetry. I spent the years 2010 and 2011 in Bologna, using the resources of its university, which at that time was one of the few with extensive material on Italian translingual writers. I worked with Hajdari to translate his poetry, meeting with him in Frosinone and elsewhere to discuss his work.

It has been just over a decade since I started this project, and though much has changed in the world, Hajdari's devotion to poetry and his resolute loyalty to its power have remained an unchanging inspiration. We all feel lost at times, and if this sense of dislocation is a side-effect of being human, then the figure of the exile is its highest expression. Hajdari's mournful, limpid poems place us inside our divided lives and press on the tender spot of our own feelings of homelessness. Hajdari

---

[1] From the poem 'Rise Jesus, Take up Your Lash'

is a master at evoking not only the lost world of a country left behind in political turmoil, but also the loss, shared by all, of the country of childhood. His work goes further still to evoke the loss of a distant, mythic sense of belonging that can never be recaptured.

The world should have given ear to Hajdari long ago. And yet, Hajdari the poet seems to understand that the very prophet (as he sometimes designates his poetic "I") who carries the most urgent message is the one most likely to be ignored. Nonetheless, his appearance in this volume to a wider Anglophone audience is timely. The painful reality of our time in which whole peoples and nations must relocate, abandon their lands, give up their war-torn countries, and find a new life is ever more painfully present.

Alice Loda speaks masterfully of Hajdari's poetics in the Afterword of this volume, but I would like to indicate to the reader a few facets of his work that are dear to me, as well as a few that bear directly on the process of translation. Hajdari's sensibility is unique and difficult to classify. Certainly he is the inheritor of the epic tradition of Albania, as he is the inheritor of the Italian poets in whose work he steeped himself as a young exile. He adds to these traditions a poetics all his own, honed through the years of his wandering exile. At times he speaks with the spare and original voice of a true lyric poet. At others, he is the mouthpiece of ancient song rooted in the long, uninterrupted Albanian oral tradition. Other times he embodies the political poet, preserving the names and places where injustice and violence occurred so that we cannot turn the blind eye we so often resort to. In another mood we find in him the troubadour love poet who stands at the headwaters of modern poetry, praising his beloved. These multiple, shifting, and overlapping identities make the translation of Hajdari's work a wonderful challenge.

One aspect that I have worked particularly to preserve is the repetition that marks Hajdari's work. The reader will notice that the same terms appear and reappear in different combinations and contexts throughout his oeuvre. In this sense, his poetry resembles a grand fugue in which certain themes and motifs surface and resurface many times. Each time these "melodies" come back to our ear, they return to us changed and inflected by the developing music that surrounds them. The repetition amplifies the significance and scope of each term over the course of the piece, or in this case, the poet's oeuvre. This structure mirrors Hajdari's life as an exile. Indeed, the musical term "fugue" (or "fuga", in Italian) means *flight*. The melodies "flee" through the piece, gaining meaning through time as they search for – or give up on – a new home.

The pastoral images of his poetic landscape are juxtaposed with a constant return to concepts such as the abyss, the void, and the beyond. The intimacy of the concrete with the abstract is one of the triumphs of Hajdari's work. Once again, it creates an image of memory and of exile. Memory contains the vivid particulars of the past, but they are untethered, free of their original context, both liberated and lost. Hajdari's work thus creates a poignant sense of what it is to be human: we are a creature that finds its expression in the body and the physical world, and yet we have the imaginative capacity to conceive of nothingness itself.

Because of their translingualism, the poems already contain the kind of distance that translation usually brings to a work. To preserve this, I have sometimes chosen to emphasize unintuitive or odd language in my translation. I have tried to do this skillfully, so that the poems maintain their integrity while at the same time nodding to the complexity that arises from their birth in two languages. At times, Hajdari asks Italian to embody – or at least clothe – uniquely Albanian aspects of his thought, whether they are native flora and fauna, mythic concepts, or, more abstractly, the linguistic texture characteristic of the epic Albanian rhapsodes of his bloodline. At others, he purposefully distances himself from his native tongue in order to write toward or about it. Hajdari sometimes uses Italian to chastise his mother tongue and his country: *"you bore me/to be your wound"*[2] he says in one poem. There are also moments in which he seems to feel permanently alienated by his existence in his second language: "I'm living in place of myself now" he says in another poem.

Yet these melancholy comments on exile are balanced by a kind of liberation that comes with rootlessness. After he imagines, in one poem, that his books will one day start a fire in the house of two cold lovers, he says *"To feel/ a little bit oneself / a little bit the universe"*.[3] It is

---

[2] From the poem that begins "Mia patria," in *Bitter Grass*.

[3] From a the poem that begins "Farsi polvere" in *Pèligorga*, not included in this collection.

a moving articulation of the kind of happiness Hajdari has preserved and fought for: the elusive, transforming self appears both within and without, present and distant, one's own as well as part of the greatest whole. Hajdari's poetry understands that though the self may sometimes appear to be a prison, it is also the key to liberation. His verse is always in the process of becoming; the death of any part of the poet signals the beginning of something else: "*With the point of the knife on my trembling skin I write/songs of love and pain. Everything becomes sound, gesture, gold*[4]." From salt and heart to gesture and gold, I am so deeply glad that more readers will now be able to experience the hospitality and the transformational power of Hajdari's work.

Sarah Stickney
St. John's College
Santa Fe, New Mexico

---

[4] From the poem that begins "Why did you cause me to be born Albanian, blind, and without memory?" in *Inside me Grows a Foreign Man.*

from
BITTER GRASS

Bitter Grass was written in 1976 while I was in my last year of high school in the Albanian city of Lushnje. It was not published by the regime's official publisher "N. Frashëri," of Tirana. According to the censor "the texts of the collection do not concern the theme of our socialist village; the hero of the poems is a solitary boy who flees from his classmates, from the Association of Pioneers, and from reality. His verses also do not include the transformations that socialism has brought to the countryside under the rule of the Party…" At that time the collection was titled *Diary of the Wood*. I translated these texts into Italian in 1999. Two years later, in 2001, the work was published for the first time by Fara Editore. This new publication has been expanded and includes new texts. To offer my readers these verses is to return many years into the past, to the cold and inhospitable winter of the Albanian dictatorship where my poetic journey began.

[Author's note]

*

No one knows if I'm still hanging on
in this scorched corner of earth
or if drunk in the depths of night I write
verses dark and joyful.

I dream of death each time
spring returns.
My groans fade to nothing
in the naked rain.

My youth is burning up
in a hurry, without echo!
All around me smile
roses and knives.

Soon my body will smell
of smoke and alcohol.
Who knows what strange fate
will someday break my voice.

*

They'll find me in the harvested fields –
no breath between my lips,
stretched out on the straw I loved,
doves pecking beside me.

My mother's white handkerchief on my face,
they'll carry me to the room I was born in:
Standing around my body people will say
"Poor boy, he suffered so much!"

After they've washed the body
with fresh well-water,
they'll put me on the grain wagon
drawn by country oxen.

One last time I'll travel
the road I ran on as a boy.
That night the fireflies
will light my new home.

*

Even from beyond the grave
your dawn curse will ring
in my ears: "you'll never be lucky,
may you die like a dog!"

I'll remember with fear
my cruel God,
the pomegranate split open
under the full moon.

The duck who dove into the lake,
the bloody towers.
The sad omen
of a wolf's cry in the dark.

Starlings drilling into the rock
as if they'd gone mad,
black thorns I plucked out with a needle
from the feet of my mother.

*

Hanging from a nail
my country school-boy satchel,
a white cloud sits on the poplar
slashed by old lightning.
Traces of my hilltop birthplace
disappear little by little –
the pomegranate garden
where our dog gave birth
hasn't felt my foot since.
I don't have a single photo
of the poor, flint cottage
where I trembled and rose early.
The mulberry bush in the red hedge
has dried up, and the old well in the courtyard,
where butterflies used to flock
morning and evening, is silent.
A clever owl wanders the elms
predicting rain or remembering sunshine.
Alas, I wander and no one
sees me. Flocks of black birds rise
from the olive trees,
the grey day
weights their wings like pain.

*

Tormented now I wander the country
like a stabbed ghost.
Death no longer scares me,
nor the cold of evening.

I know who loved me
in the delirious hills.
An eternal love:
the mud and the winter dark.

Behind me destiny
trails like a shadow.
As a nightcap I choose
snake-bite.

I'm taking two things with me
to the promised land:
the cries of prey in springtime
and the songs of gypsies.

*

Nothing dawns
on time's face.

The Balkan night –
black leather.

The valley's abyss
holds the dust of my wishes,
the ashes of my seasons.

What am I looking for
on the dark hilltop
of this tormented country
of drunkards?

In our garden the wind
knocks quinces down into mud
like ugly dreams.

*

Immense like you, hill,
my anguish.
Every burning verse you inspire in me
is love and torment.

I have never been so free
since your summit with the *xhin*.[5]
I will always remember
I am the creation
of your wild sin.

Dreams and hopes flee into nothing
at the first touch of cold.
Realms of passion and ruins
invite my body.

Under the olive tree
my shadow calls.
A dark flame at the horizon
burns cries and voices.

---

[5] Xhin, pronounced 'gin', are malevolent spirits which come out at night and have a supernatural power over people and things. The legend comes from Albanian fairy tales of Darsìa, but the word xhin is also related to the Arabic *djinn*, and thus has connotations of 'genie' and other supernatural creatures of Arabic literature.

*

We'll walk the dew-white morning
through the empty forest.
The scent of yellow leaves
wakes in you a distant childhood.

In the middle of thick-limbed elms
you're first to find the path.
At your brow turtle doves
and in your hands blackbirds pause.

You count the trunks
of broken trees in silence,
remembering their features
like loved ones now dead.

Enchanted by the echoes of voices,
as quiet as thieves.
Beneath our feet lie buried
rites, sorrows, and black magic.

In your eyes wet with autumn
Escape and oblivion appear.
Lost in the night forest
we won't find our way back.

*

Often in the depths of night
a strange voice enters my room,
it always appears at the same time
out of a deep well's darkness.

It sits next to my bed
somber and menacing.
How many times I have woken
in worry and fear!

"Don't be frightened young man–
it repeats every time in the dark –
the shadows who appear in your dreams,
are not chimeras.

You will live a long life as a warrior[6]
among vipers and crows.
Your only traveling companions will be
thorns and stones.

Go forward on your road,
pay no attention to false oracles.
Your farmer's seed
will be engraved in the Albanian mud."

Then it vanishes into the dark
to the bottom of the deep well,
only to return each night at the same time,
ever more somber and menacing.

---

[6] warrior for peace

*

No one can ever know
what will happen to my world.
In the company of thunder and lightning
I'll travel the winter nights.

I look around me. Everything goes silent.
Mud becomes one with the eternal.
In vain I search the horizon for someone
to trust with my fate.

Long shadows wind around
my hands, feet, brain.
I don't know if I'll have a future
in this harsh, blood-stained bloodline.

*

I don't care
what my fate brings me.
If something grim is lurking
I don't want to know about it.

I've lived so long
in my terror.
I've wandered the streets of Hajdaraj[7]
like my tomb.

I know what's waiting for me
behind the veil of dusk.
In this world of knives
I'm not asking to be saved.

---

[7] Hajdaraj is the name of the village where the author was born. It is situated to the north-east of the city of Lushnje, in the province of Darsìa.

*

Moon,
this season too has fled
kissless
into the sleepless night.

Sky,
this year too has passed
without explanation,
the dried-up well's thirst
on our black lips.

Valley,
even this century is leaving
like a beaten bull,
time slipping through its fingers
and the cuckoo's song that calls
from hill to hill.

*

Don't despair
because the valley is sad
and the forest without echo in the dusk.

Wind scatters
the ashes from spent fires
on the hilltop.

Don't despair,
remember: I'm here beside you
hiding in the green.

*

Don't cry,
it's the robin who runs
on the iced river.

Soon the almond tree will bloom
and songbirds will sing about it
in our veins.

Don't cry
I travelled the length of your wound
to reach you.

*

Chasing the cuckoo through
bushes of blooming broom,
Listening at dusk to the call of the robin
motionless on the hawthorn's bare branch.

Remembering the voice of those who leave,
blending with the light sorrow of passersby
and with the scent of ripe wheat fields.

Studying the hill, lights and shadows,
the trembling of the thin horizon line which burns
even from the beyond with your green eyes.

*

At the bottom of the garden our old well whitens with age,
from the branches of the willow tree birds seldom sing,
even the bucket has ceased to sound on the stones
as it moves up and down, its rope,
worn thin by hands, has snapped.

Voices and footsteps have been lost
and the path that led there is covered with mallow.
In the water's mirror, as in the old days,
I wait in vain for my mother's face to appear.

*

My country,
why this crazy love for you?

You bore me
to be your wound.

Where can I hide
on the barren hill

My verses follow me
like old murderers.

Deep in my ice, every night
something breaks.

*

This evening I want someone to call me from the stones,
this evening I want to get out of my Darsìa
in the rain.

I want to look into the face of my cruel god,
this evening I want the earth to drink
my red blood
and hide my last word.

This evening, my country, I want out.

From

RAIN ANTHOLOGY

Rain Anthology was written in the '80s. It was delivered to the regime's publisher Naim Frashëeri in Tirana in 1985 and was not published. According to the censor of the Albanian regime, "The literary principles of the reality of socialism are not reflected here. Furthermore, a positive hero is absent as is the guiding role of the Party in the day to day life of the country and of the people and their awareness of communism." The collection was finally published in November of 1990, two months before the dictatorship fell. The first self-translated edition was published in Italian in 2000 with the publisher Fara. The second Italian edition came out in 2018 with Edizioni Ensemble. This new publication was expanded to include texts that, for ideological reasons, were not in the first editions. To offer readers this collection of verses brings alive in me the distant years I lived in terror under the communist dictatorship of Enver Hoxha.

[Author's note]

*

I now believe in nothing!
Do you hear me, my curved earth?

I'm scared of my Shadow
and of your empty world.

I turn to you
shadow of my shadow
and I call on you
as tomorrow's judge.

Often my thoughts are gloomy
for those dead
and for those still living
like the bitter grass
that keeps
its balance.

I say to myself: who knows
what fate
(in a time robbed of fate)
these visible things will have!

*

Here in rain's homeland
a thin thread separates us.

Those still here
wear the faces
of those who are leaving.

*

Maybe the barren hills of Darsìa
will lock up my fragile lines
under the black thorns of pomegranate trees
pierced by freezing eastern winds.

Far from the love of maidens
who will never know their torment,
they'll remain alone under the black sky
like a robin in the dark
of winter.

Grass swish and blackbird song
will keep their lament company.
While the short fall nights'
pale moon will cover them.

*

Is it true that in your heart
I'm a nail, memory, ache,
black lip, the cold under your skin
that laughs and cries like a madman?

Tell me what I am: a spiteful angel
who stands in shrubs and bogs
ripping up my own fate
and flinging mud on Christ and Mohammed?

Or am I the fire in the fatal dark
hidden in bad dreams
that seduces and torments
with a sweet and terrible face?

Your silence digs into my brain
exhausted by the immense night.
Smiling, I contemplate you under the moon
like a soldier examining his wound.

*

I'm witness to your ancient cry
and to those who called you and rejected you.
You're searching in the dark, wide eyed,
for what, chimera of clay and blood?

How many times I've seen you weep, evenings
dragging your life through the cold.
I ran to you shoeless and frightened,
and I caressed your shadowy forehead.

You are the voice that lacerates my thirsty flesh
which burns in the fire of your forest.
There's no poison to calm our passions
on this mad, barren hill.

*

Stony, closed skies
where you appear and are lost.

Sterile territories
where sprouts
the shadow of your body.

*

Beside me nothing flows,
I am still me.
I remember only myself
in the aging mud.

*

Nights as black as dog's eyes
hang before the closed doors
that line the border of barbed wire.

Marble statues
false oracles
abysses.

Cruel fate wanted me
to be born in this village of drunks
where they nail me up every day
in the name of the people.

The ripped belly of the stony earth
gathers in silence the martyred bodies
of those "enemies" of the country
with the bullets confiscated at the front.

*

At the top of the hill
drunken farmers,
call of voices,
black of mountains.

Beyond the valley where the *xhin*
hide in the shadow of stones,
yesterday repeats itself
tiredly as today.

Along the border of barbed wire
the bitter grass has lost its balance.

*

Stepmother land, fate foretold by the memory
of my vengeful bloodline,
I offer myself to you as an animal wounded by the claws
of its prey after the last battle
in death's arena.

May your evil will be done
and your children feed on blood.

Far away my solitary flock flees
across mournful seasons,
dried out springs, ruins, and gods
that illuminate no truth.

*

If Spring beats you to Kupas,
tell me
and I'll wait for it at the border that divides our provinces.

And if that morning
I happen to be listening
to Mozart's requiem,
I'll leave my house early
I'll put on my blue shirt
with the short sleeves,
the one my neighbor sewed,
I'll run through the frosted fields
like a madman,
I'll whistle one of the old songs
and I'll see my face in the flowing waters.

I'll see my face in the flowing waters,
in the mirror of lakes
the shadow of the day
the clouds floating away
over the barbed wire
and the return of the storks.

I'll close my brown eyes
and I'll hear birdsong,
the voices of our martyred earth.

And you, my love, you won't recognize me
because I have become green and sound.

I've quit being me.

*

All your tragedy, History,
has fallen on me. I'm worried.
My light body can't support
its gloomy weight.

How long will this merciless circle
of shadow stretch over everything?
With its hungry bites it devours
the living and the dead.

I imagine those who will climb
to the dark hilltop. Obsessed.
Like me they will try to live
in memory or oblivion.

In the dark my silhouette moves,
falls, and gets up muddy.
The way a ghost in old tales
fights the god of shadows.

From

DOG SHADOW

*

A blind verse
without memory –
that's my body,
born in a poor country.

———————————

*

Mother,
I've lost metaphors.

———————————

*

What am I waiting for in this empty room?

———————————

*

It rains constantly
in this
country.

Maybe because I'm a stranger.

---

*

Ever more alone here in the West
I
and my body.

---

*

Where's your holiness Rome,
where's your sea?
Even the rivers have disappeared;
pain is heard only in the water
                 of fountains.
These visible things,
                 innocent,
this sky full of signs
like the eyes of the women
                 in via del Corso,
these days all alike
frighten me.
Everyone's in flight
as they follow a rough fate
towards deserts of monsters,
deserts beyond
other deserts.

---

*

How sad they are
these cities
with man dead inside them

From

STONES WINDWARD

*

Will there be other possibilities?

---

*

Who's that singing in the fog?
I recognize you as you emerge from the river
with your cold, marble lips,
but I won't call your name.
Afterwards you'll be called by others
who come from yet more winter.
I'm leaving for the void
to cry out for the blood spilled
in this sterile place.

---

*

We smell the smell of blood.
The dog who whimpers on the sand hill
is the call of the dead.
For years we've walked without rest
breathing our silence.
The black line of birds leads us,
so we can flee beyond the borders
of this maddened place.

---

*

This closed sky
won't carry you to the realm of the living.
Far away, time
flows under the snow's skin.
You leave us, leaving the empty space
where your trembling body stood
and the lament of the dead.
Where you're going they're not waiting
for you, and you'll find no one, nothing
except the snake's hiss
and the stones of that country they call winter.

---

*

Nothing remains of those dreams,
the houses stand locked for good.
Under the stones
you won't find a single key;
they brought them along, the dead.

---

*

We get lost in the mist
like bodies in the abyss
of time. Stones lock up
the sky, and that's not the sun
that shines, but gravestones
face down in unknown suburbs.
Those who flee the snow
speak of spent fires

on the hilltop.
We notice with dismay
the tombs of the dead are empty:
no bones no names.
Behind trees and statues
packed tightly together
rise shadows of blood,
images of dust.
Impatiently, someone
asks for the next home
on this earth that breathes.

---

*

Forgetting we are blind
we leave by night
to reach a naked place
that needs our voice.
We're going to the sea to talk
and throw stones windward.

---

*

No other gesture is possible.

From

BODY PRESENT

*

I sing my body present
born of this cold space
that promises nothing.

At night
visions of white temples
call me to the void.

I dreamed of lonely fields
as I look for vague signs
and understand the sky's mask
which longs for the abyss.

I don't know why I stare
at the thin horizon line
or the barren peaks with their black birds.

That thing I can't find
is it hiding
in the waving algae
or white lichens?

I go forward through the burnt-up green
and I bring nothing except my body.

I'll leave nothing!

*

I'm a bell of the sea
of silences, of voices –
I'm closed into time.

No god hears the sounds
of water and fire
in my flesh.

In the West
every spring that arrives
is a wound that reopens.

Hollowed by shadows and stones,
I spend the Italian nights
in a gurgle of blood.

Years in fear of death.

Tricked by oracle voices
I call out to familiar faces
who don't – and never will – return!

Sterile my dreams
in the dark of my empty room.

Every day I go slightly more mad.

*

By now this country's language
is useless;
it brings disaster
to trees and birds.

In this part of the world
we live by words of stone
and by the glory of words.

We dig down into our bodies
to hide
with the cold clouds
of the valley.

We'll never be free
like the hills!

*

Those who continue to flee in the snow
turning their backs
on diminished skies
and fragile walls that shake,
are in the power of unknown homes
and of pale moons at night.

Why are they driven to burn memories,
and abandon nostalgia?

And the ashes of the dead, the deserted altars,
what will become of them?

Turn towards the call from beyond the border,
bless the trampled flowers, the water from the wells
where you quenched your thirst.

They will protect you during your exile
among enchanting forests
and pitiless seasons.

*

We are here among stones
with stones
surrounded by cold in the fields
and by the big eyes of crows,
waiting to hear a voice
come to us from the sandy camps
that are covered by dark clouds.

In our pockets we carry the list of the dead
and days in a naked place
without cries or memories.

Mouths shut tight hide our words,
we push walls of wind
to see on the other side
the black lips of the river
we heard about in old stories.

*

We cling to our names
ripped out like grass

and we don't know where it comes from,
this loneliness.

Maybe we should have stayed
closer to the memory of trees
or overturned statues.

For years we've been walking
the barren fields
without childhood.

A slow snow
falls over our bodies

*

We can't find a way to speak
with these skies nailed over us.

Our language dresses in the clothes
of another language that sprouts
crows,
crows that fly over ice and wrecked walls.

Even the fires back home
won't surrender us to the new fires
we still need badly.

*

September is the month
you reappear among new trees
next to old stones.

You walk on leaves
that continue
to bleed.

This time you arrive from the forest
wrapped in hymns and silences.
You aren't covered in rain,
you come to speak.

Under your skin you carry loneliness,
despair in your blood.

Rivers and woods follow your body
to give you a life that doesn't die.

*

What exists outside
is waiting, simply,
thirsty for snow
like me.

*

In the valley

sterile sand will remain
plowed by the snake.

Trees stand tightly together
like in hunger years.

The words they shout to the sky
inflame the language
of the living.

Tracing the edge of disaster
man and beast go
united in silence
and in space,

until they reach
a land that is parched,
inhospitable.

*

I'll remain
like dog shadow
bitter grass
throwing stones windward
in the foreign nights.

Hemmed in by invasive ivy
by damp shivers
in the bare room.

Unmoving
like the black of mountains
stroked by cutting rain.

My deconsecrated body will also remain
with your name that met the night,
the death of light.

*

How sad Rome is
without you my love
without your eyes
your lips
(blood red)
your shadow.

Next to me
you're like a hill
a field of grain
or virgin forest
where rain knocks
and the world
knocks too.

If you call
angels answer
if you shout
the sea hears you
if you cry
the ruins will welcome you.

I lose you and regain you
through walls and caves
alive and dead
by the same stones
by the same shadows!

*

You live facing winter
like a wound. Unmoving and foreign
in this imperfect space, never welcoming,
you wait for the unbroken silence of the sand
to tell you the secret. Don't be dazed by wandering rivers
and new trees that weren't there before.
Around you the falling of things will continue,
the disappearance of poets who tie sky to earth.
It's said we will die in opposite lands. My years:
a flight into the unknown and frightened wakings at night.

*

I'm the truth
of a journey and the shadow line
guarded by the living and closed earth
that wants to hide something from us.

I live suspended
without belonging to a home,
at the crossroads of balance.

With slow steps I've walked
among the thirsty dead
to reach the next day's dawn
of fires and reprieves.

Infinity, my host,
I'm tired of time and of the void.

What is my fragment
or your fragment?

My anguish has become horizontal
like my illusions,
so thin is the wall
that defends and divides me.

*

You tell me that yesterday
you fell to the ground on your knees
ah, our ground
delirium and dust;
with your aged face
turned toward the arabian deserts
you prayed for me,
body trembling.

Thousands of kilometers, states, temples,
ice, lighting, winds
vast solitudes of sand
must be crossed by your prayer:
pure essence in substance,
to get to the Black Stone.[8]

---

[8] Black Stone: this is a reference to the Black Stone of Mecca in Saudi Arabia where faithful Muslims go to pray during the days of Ramadan.

*

The weightless extension of fields separates us,
and the highland of free swallows.

We wanted to live on mountaintops,
but the echo of valleys
did not respond to the echo of our calls.

We search for words in a different season,
in the place where our glances fell.

The faces we loved
have gone in search of a new exile
and another alphabet.

Who will recognize the blood on rocks
and in the beds of dry rivers?

That time was different,
like cricket song
in empty rooms.

Other bodies were here before us
in this parched green

New faces
now accompany our footsteps.

Evenings, we look out the window
at the line of trees
standing tightly together.

*

I fold into nothing
and hide my man's secrets.

On the hills with their spent fires
the wind makes waves
of the white sheets
of the dead.

The anonymous faces fall silent,
they don't know how to cry.

Who is there to turn to
in this sterile Country?

Like a mournful monk
I bury in the dark soil
the fallen flowers of the almond tree.

*

We take refuge in our light bodies
wrapped in the mist of this valley
that continues like bitter grass to keep its balance.

Winter fields have nothing
to say to us
and regions of ice teach us
only cold.

From now on we have to learn
how to live
like the closed sky.

*

Wherever I go in the West
I bring my hollowed face with me.

In my sad eyes,
(as in a prison),
my Albania, lost voices
and you, soaked by other rains.

Maybe one of these rainy days
I'll die too,
in the street,

killed by one of my own stones
thrown windward.

From

STIGMATA

*

I'm leaving these lines like a goodbye
swallowed by memory's nakedness
knowing the world doesn't need them.

My waving hand that trembles
down in the starry depths
is noticed by no one.

Precarious horizon
I'm leaning on your cold water
and digging into the forehead of your dark sky.

Abandoned in thick fog I don't know
where I'm coming from or where I'm going,
I attack the snows that attack me
at the mercy of black birds.

I want to know who keeps me away from the maddened land
and what will become of my shadow beyond the water,
the rain that falls in the rain
and the gods among trees.

In line next to the cold, next to fate
I'm waiting for pale faces with hoarse voices
to call me at dawn from the rocks.

My name nostalgia that divides
light from darkness,
my body the line between sand and sky.

*

This evening I'm waiting for the border-snow
for the sea of sand, for the faces in the water to calm me.
There's no other sky where I can drown my frenzy:
everywhere the night of men who die.

My terror, where can I stop?
The stones I threw windward
have opened a great abyss above me.

Now time makes a home in time
and I cross room after room, wall after wall.
I'm an exile exiled in exile
with blood scattered over trees and a voice in the rain.

Do you know my pain? I walk alongside those
who trace the edge that catches fire.

Go forward, go forward black eagles with two heads, devour each part
of my lacerated body, hang my red heart from the branches,
drink my blood like starving beasts
bury my songs
leave me only the time to cover
this ordinary childhood.

Alas, in the riverbeds the future
in the black of the world the past.

*

I listen to my silence. I am frightened
of dying in another language,
in this cold that doesn't belong to me.

I'll disappear into the abyss of my verses
where eternal calls invite me,
pierced by the rain of exile.

*

How poor we are.
In Italy I live hand to mouth,
at home you can't even afford a black coffee.

Our crime: we love,
our sentence: to live alone divided
by the dark water.

I'll come back in autumn like Constantine,[9]
in our native hills you will already
have gathered oregano
for me to take back to my still-bare room.

I'm living in place of myself now
far away from that land that pitilessly
devours its own children.

---

[9] Constantine: also known as the 'Rider of Death', this is a character in the most beautiful canto of the song cycle of the Albanian people of Italy (*Arbëresh*), that has as its main motif the *besa*.

*

River, you must tell how I was also here
like the grain in the fields, the wild rose in the dark woods.
I lived like you – always wearing damp clothes,
starving for existence, enchanted by the summer sunflower
in a strange century during which people
walked looking down.
I passed evenings of cutting rain alone
behind wet glass in the west.
I thought of creating with yesterday's knife
another homeland of rock
in my trembling Eastern body.

*

That's my skin hanging from the wind and ringing
with its announcement of blood-smeared bulls in the summer fields,
fireflies of passion in deconsecrated temples.

That's my childhood of stigmata that calls out
as it lies on the ashes of spent fires
dreaming of poppies and the hissing of vipers along pathways.

That's my fate: confined to the dusk I listen
and look for my voice in the mist
of another alphabet.

*

Every day I create a new homeland
in which I die and am reborn,
a country without maps or flags
celebrated in those deep eyes
of yours that follow me for the whole length
of my journey towards fragile skies.
In all lands I sleep as one in love,
in all homes I wake up as a child,
my key can open every border
and the doors of every black prison.
Eternal returns and departures my being
from fire to fire, water to water.
The national anthem of my country: the blackbird's song
that I sing in every season of the waning moon.
It is born out of your forehead of darkness and stars
with the eternal will of the sun god.

*

In which season do I seek you
from which rock do I call you
over which snows do you walk.

You're what remains in me of a summer night,
insomnia, little death and peace,
green grass growing in the burned fields.

In you the light rises, the dark descends,
I cover you with broom flowers and blackbird songs,
along the pathways of your fingers
move days present and future.

In whatever language you dream yourself you are the same: body and time,
as in days of old you sing your childhood: from hill to hill;
let it move across you like a goatherd with his goats.

*

Returning to Ciociaria in full May
I see the broom flowering
and cry.

Everywhere in the valley sounds, lights, and shadows.

Springtime, when you arrive in exile
I try to resist.

I lie down on the bitter grass
to gaze at the sky, the void,
while memories fill up the distance.

*

When you disembarked at the port of Trieste it was April, nine o'clock
in the evening. Like today it was raining on the city and the castle.
The bora swept away dreams and nocturnal birds,
I brought with me sadness: land without name
and manuscripts rolled quickly into a white handkerchief.

There were two of us: myself and your eyes that have followed me
since who knows when into oblivion,
I walked distracted in the steps of Saba[10].
The sea caves and you, in secret, predicted my destiny
of rusty borders.

Trieste, I was your saddest man that evening
raised with love for the apricot tree
and stork-flight over the fields,
in flight from the East in springtime,
at night
defeated,
in the rain,
without a handshake.

---

[10] Umberto Saba (1883–1957): Italian poet

*

For you men of Europe who make do every day,
for you women of the East who wash floors
or take the old people of the west out for fresh air,
for you immigrants who sleep on benches and awake
with immense nostalgia,
for you drunkards who want no bosses
and live in peace with the universe,
for you prostitutes who offer your sex to people black, white,
and yellow until you bleed,
for you blind abandoned in deepest eternal darkness,
for you sick and unemployed, like solidarity and mercy,
for you missionaries who bring consolation to the weak
before they die,
for you farmers who take the flock to pasture and plough
the fields from north to south,
for you mad who teach us madness for free,
for you who are alone and flee like me
I write these verses in Italian
and torment myself in Albanian.

*

I often dream of returning to the hills of Judas Trees
to live next to you,
let poverty come and be welcome
as long as I'm next to you.
Years have passed since they forced me to go away.

What are you doing? What do you think? Will we be saved in this life?

The fate of poets is hard,
yesterday we were dangerous for the dictatorship,
today we are useless for liberty.

Ah, if only I had loved a woman from the village
I wouldn't have suffered so much in the cities that kill,
where I must defend myself every second.

Write me if you've heard the song of the cuckoo
in the blooming broom.

*

My body shakes,
my blood dances,
my veins sing,
I'm no longer myself.
I burn little by little
like wax in a temple abandoned in a hurry,
I lose myself little by little
in time's abyss.
I have in my hands the nests of the *peligorga*[11]
in my eyes, your snows.
If you see deserts, they grow on my skin,
if you see lightning, it enters my flesh,
if you see murderers, they surround my heart.
I've never been so amazed at myself.

---

[11] *Peligòrga* is a solitary green-feathered bird which frequents the borders of rivers and streams. It nests in the earth, and can be found near Darsìa, the hilly province where the poet was born.

*

I am a man of the border
wounded in my wound
in love with Nothing
and the origin of cold.

I'm a man who lives on little
condemned by the borders
to the borders.

My eyes are crossroads
between the ones who arrive
and the others who leave.

Inside myself I'm a little no one
and a little everyone,
drunk on worlds.

From

BLACK THORNS

*

You all came here to live next to me in the West
tired and bent
like the willows of our country.

You brought with you a bundle of tea from Mount Tomorr[12]
and you wore your old wool clothes
that you wear winter and summer,
it's all that remains to you in this life.

Martyred Darsìa, we turned our backs on you
like a ripped shirt
hanging from the pomegranate's bloody thorns.

How much I feared this might happen.

---

[12] The highest mountain in the southwest of Albania, where tea is grown.

*

One day we will also become Darsìa,
one day we'll become its sky of clouds and birds,
its trees, its bitter grass, its sweet smell of forever.

The loneliness that penetrates our bones
like winter damp
will dry up.

The seasons will have our voices,
the days will have our eyes on the altar,
others will speak our bloody language.

We'll pass beyond time
under the profane eye of the day
as we distance ourselves from our names.

*

The hill of Judas Trees, the sea thundering at the horizon
before rain, the lightning and the dark clay
that stuck to my swollen, cold feet,
all these will peer out of your dreams during the foreign nights.

How will you manage to wake up
without the rooster's song in the mulberry branches.

The countryside full of black thorns
where you worked barefoot
will knock every evening on your soul's door.

*

I want my body to rest far from the homeland
and my ashes to be scattered elsewhere.

*

Don't forget the river,
we got lost there.

On its banks, when you go,
you'll find my face
suspended in the water.

Call me,
my voice will respond from where it's strewn on the grass,
hidden among the willows.

*

You announce springtime
and the end of war
when you arrive from the vineyard or the sea.

Your mouth the scent of peach,
your forehead the height of new moons.

You have the eyes of a blackbird.
How will I get you out of my mind
you call to me in your southern voice.

Look on my behalf at the green, the lights, the shadows
knowing that return is useless.

You announce springtime
and the end of war
when you arrive from the vineyard or the sea.

BLACK THORNS

There was once a thin boy with a fragile soul
and brown eyes with a piercing gaze like that of a black crow,
born in a magical winter of seaside thunder and lightning
raised on the bare hill near burning stars.

When he saw the first pale rays of sun:
"His name will live eternally – said the lakes and blind fogs
from stone into stone his verb will be sculpted,
and his story will be narrated down the centuries."

"O women, we will make him immortal –
swore the elves in the dark valleys –
we will teach him the language of the grouse and the fairies
and we will entrust him to love."

For seven days and seven nights he slept in the wings of the Ore
without eating or suckling at the breast of a woman.
It was a pact made with his mother
if the creature was born a boy.

With a beautiful name they baptized him in his native country of sages
who arrived from the land of the star and crescent.
With fresh well-water those gypsy women blessed him one February
          morning
with their hollow faces and their black braids.

He came from the east, the land where the sun is born,
he spent his childhood among rites and falcons.
He made broom-flower garlands for his goat
and twined them around its old horns.

"We'll call him the noble title of Bey
and we will increase his lands – his paternal grandparents toasted him –
first he will become the prince of his people
and afterward the king of the country."

Years passed and he grew on the milk of swallows
the sun dried the thorns of his future crown,
the forest enlarged the trunk of his throne white as snow,
in the lunar fields fertile rains fell.

In his country the wind was always blowing and the grass grew curved
while at night on the banks of the river beautiful brides danced.
His ancient bloodline was born of blood feuds,
healers of snake-bite and seers of future destiny were his forebears.

Over the mud and thorns his humble people walked
with hope in the earth and the blessing of the Father.
When someone died, he was buried in the shade of the olive tree
without cross or star and crescent.

So it was that the boy in secret at night
decided to descend from the hill to the deep river
waiting frightened in the silent dark
to meet the beautiful dancing brides.

"O handsome young man – they said to him when they saw him –
tell us what good fortune has brought you here? –
while they danced all around him
linked by their braids.

No one has ever dared to attend
our nocturnal dance under the full moon
may your seed never grow on this earth
you are eternally cursed.

You will die in exile of heartbreak
far from your severe bloodline.
Stones and two-headed black eagles
will devour your weak flesh without mercy.

No one will ever pronounce your name
in daily talk no one will call it out.

Mournful sin will weigh on you
like an old nail stuck in your forehead.

Your soul will never be loved
no woman will shelter your body.
You'll live forgotten by the world
like a stone thrown to the side of the road!"

So into the dark river the white brides disappeared
singing and dancing in the language of rivers.
Whirlwinds of fire enveloped the boy seven times
leaving no sign of blood nor wounds.

Starting that deep night
the spirits abandoned our valleys.
Women wore black shawls over their heads
a disquiet dirge was heard through the land.

The lightning ceased and the seaside thunder,
the roosters in the land sang day and night.
Drought and thorns grew in the seeded fields
Shadows reigned everywhere.

One rainy day he crossed the sea
wrapped in seasons and blind fogs.
He felt as though someone were following him into oblivion
as if they wanted to stab him.

Nothing is known of his wanderer's life,
his mysteries are enclosed in the depths.
Like a mournful monk he flees over the world
with an old shoe hung around his neck.

The legend goes like this:
it is said that at night he returns
to the land of the east that exists no more
on a white a horse.

WESTERN WORLD, WHERE IS YOUR BESA?[13]

Why do these men dressed in black
knock on my old door?
Do they come in joy or in mourning?
Why does the wind from the mountain cease,
and the nightingale stills to listen?
Tell me, what has happened to my Gëzim?
I am his mother and I must know.
Is he with you, my son?
Tell me has he perished in the street
or in his bare room
beyond the black sea in the land of Saturn?
Miserable me! What a *gjama*[14]!
– Get out of here mournful voice!
– Open the door my mother
– Who are you behind the door?
– Dear lady mother, I am Gëzim.
– Get out of here dead witch!
What do you expect in the *kulla malsore*,
return to singing, my friends:
my son is not dead but alive!
Today there is great rejoicing in Darsìa.
Tell me, what do you want, men in black?
Your silence is not a good sign,
your faces betray you!
Tell me, where is my joy?
A worse punishment God
could not have given me!
Western world, where is your *besa*
that you would return to me Gëzim saved from exile?
Alas, how you are diminished, my son!
Why these wounds from stones on your body,
why do your stigmata run blood
and why is your flesh full of black thorns?

---

[13] Besa: pledge or word of honor in Albanian culture.

[14] Gjama: a ceremony of grief, tragedy, funeral lament.

How the West has massacred you, Gëzim!
Welcome to your hills, welcome!
Welcome to your Darsìa
of which you sang so much!

Now your body will tremble no more
now you are immobile in the ice of death!
Miserable me, my dear son, bereft of you,
of your proud eyes now lightless,
of your mouth without a thread of voice.
I will bury you at the top of the bare hill
in the dawn under the full moon,
your mother will guard your tomb
and she will bury there her heart also,
my hope, you are tired you need to sleep.
Speak, Gëzim, to your mother
who is dying with exhaustion,
today your dear old mother will marry you
to the dancer in the river
the one you always dreamed about.
I want you to have many children
so they can be near, can help.
Now we have our land
we'll grow grain and sunflowers
we'll go down to the market every Sunday
like we used to do, we sold melons
and bursting pomegranates,
we'll build a new house with stones of flint,
we'll have goats and chickens.

– My cuckoo bird listen to me
I want to leave you an *amanet*:
run flying to Hajdàraj
and tell three words to Nur[15]:
I don't want any crying in the house
nor mourning from those who loved me.

---

[15] Nur: name of the poet's mother.

– What a beautiful *nur* wraps your face,
you've never been so handsome my Gëzim,
sleep my light, sleep my death
the journey has been long,
exile hard, the West cruel.
I'll wake you early tomorrow,
your father won't bite off your head anymore
like he did thirty five years ago
when you lost a sheep in the pasture.

– Oh moon in the sky your splendor you dimmed,
why didn't you nod that night?
I would have hastened to the West
I would have joined my son,
perhaps he did not want me by his side.
Curses upon you traitor moon:
you saw him fall and you stayed silent!

– Calm yourself my dear old mother,
I am alive and right hear next to you,
it was only a bad dream.
If my fate is to be so short
I won't leave this world
without your blessing!

From

MOONACHE

*

The stillness of your body without masks or false altars
where inscriptions and new fires spring forth. I expect nothing from
       my verses
whose wandering fate lies in the shadow of knives
in a world that drowns in gloryless idols.
Wherever I go, through cities and bazaars, they recognize me.
The stigmata left deep marks on my face and in my flesh
like wagon wheels in autumn fields after rain,
like the branding iron of the concentration camps on the skin of
       the deported.
O maiden of the North, you come down from hills tinged with sunset,
the springs of your red lips won't draw my days anymore,
you remind me of the call of crows in the New England woods
and the wren of my farming province on the coast of *gjama*.

*

To return to the border I had to cross my wound
that borders your wound that still wounds me,
climbing over waning moons fallen on the Alabama cotton fields,
wet with sweat and with the blood of African blacks,
bought at auction in Texas for ten dollars.
I charge you to make ready the return of my ashes
from your north to my south,
ashes light as summer dew
swollen with shouts and desperation.
Ashes in love with light searching for the voice of my ancestors
in the darkness of the ancient stones.
And if you come to the Balkans, blinded by the *gjama*,
you'll find my orphan childhood trembling in the wind
like snakeskin hanging from a bush.

*

Take me to my homeland
where no one expects me.
My bloody homeland
beaten like a beast knifed in the forehead.
My homeland stabbed in the back,
of trees standing tight together,
my homeland of surrendered borders, without provisions from your North.
Scatter me from hill to hill at day's end,
sow me in the fields and on the breasts of maidens
in love with the full moon in summer.
Touch me with your white hands,
read my ashes with your superior Tongue.
Leave me at the entrance of pathways into the dark woods,
the blackbird with his yellow beak will recognize me, and the *peligorga*
       in the valley.
When the spring sprouts, under the beacon of the lighthouse,
you'll see the wild rose growing out of my ashes,
the song of the cuckoo,
the fresh thorns of the hawthorn.

*

I told you my best book
would be written by knife-point
on my skin with its stigmata,
remember, it was March – the Judas Trees flowered
with fear and joy at the edges of ravines.
Perhaps the best book,
rising from my ashes and resembling your life,
was the one I wrote in the bare room while I watched out the window,
witness of Time and of those returning seasons
stroked by the memory of rains.
I wrote it in extreme poverty,
in my days of pain and moonache,
distant from your voice and from your footsteps in the city,
carrying on my shoulders from one shore to the next
the books of a country that adores tyrants.

*

I've waited a long time for this day,
facing roses and maddened knives
like an assassin awaits a victim
or like the stake waits to burn the heretic,
to show you these lines without arcs of nostalgia.
They escaped death one April night in the rain.
I cut them into love's distant ruins
fertilized with the rich shadow,
born out of the burning forest of a woman
in a terrible time.
I've waited a long time for this night,
like the virgin bride her spouse
or like a field of poppies waits for bloody dawn.
Where does your body end?
And where does my madness begin?

*

For years I've lunched in Frosinone's *Mirabar* trattoria.

What I consume gets written in pencil
by the owner of the place
on a scrap of yellow paper

It gets paid at the end of the month,
when I earn a few cursed lire
from my readings around Italy.

Destiny's irony:
just like that my mother in the East
paid the shopkeeper in my native village
for our daily bread during the communist dictatorship.

*

How wonderful it is to hear your words,
how sad to hear your trembling voice,
your heartrending voice from the other coast
reaching out of the darkness with darkness.
You left the telephone
and you went out of the post office with tears in your eyes,
how many times I've seen those eyes cry,
how little you've laughed in your life.
Tonight at the top of the dark hill of Judas Trees
in the little stone cottage in the country
you won't sleep a wink,
you'll recall the time we were together.
My poor dear,
my hard fate is destroying you,
it doesn't matter that the imam didn't accept
your prayer for me,
saying that poets aren't believers.
Tell him that every poem your son writes is a prayer
and my empty room is an altar.
Don't stop dreaming
from your seat on the stone
in front of the rusty gate
of my return
from exile.

*

We've waited so long to speak
we don't know how to say anything
under the new trees,
near the old stones.
They push us to the borders of another exile,
men and beasts pressed tightly together.
What will happen to your ashes
far from the homeland?
Our voices will be lost to oblivion
along with our greying names.
Wherever we go we'll remember the song of the blackbird
in the pathways full of black thorns
and the grieving of the sea
along the other coast.

*

Ever since the rainy season arrived
I haven't written a single line,
I haven't thought about anything.
Along with grey days and blades of bitter grass
I'm also a little dead.
I walk up and down the foreign city
enjoying the sharp, autumn sun
wrapped in a light sadness.
The wind that enters from the open windows
scatters my papers around the room
and throws them into the street
like out-of-date obituaries.
In a province far from wild almond trees,
someone notes my absence
and I don't know anymore to whom I belong.

*

I don't know why I thought of you
in this peninsula of earthquakes,
my deskmate[16] from high school,
maybe because the grey of this winter noon
resembles the mud of far away Savra,
there among the whistling reeds in the low country of Tërbuf,
the muddy shade of your youth still wanders.
I recall once again our words from that time
like birds of light in the tyrannical Albanian night.
I first read you my verses *The blood-smeared bulls*
during history class,
sitting in the desk furthest to the back.
Your boots full of holes contained a lifetime passed in internment camps;
in my broken farmer's shoes were blades of bitter grass.
How can I forget your squalid shed,
you son of an 'enemy' of the people
where, terrified you read for the first time
the poetry of D'Annunzio.
Just like today it rained terror and mud.

---

[16] Dedicated to the poet Jozef Radi, a high-school classmate who, together with his parents, was forced to spend forty years in the swampy fields Tërbuf and in the deportation camps of Kuç, Rodostinë, Çermë and Savër.

WILD ROSE

*

Along moon-covered pathways
I'm led by a flute's echo
that even in fear enchants and seduces.

*

Your flute
in the strange nights
a requiem.

*

Your flute
goodbye to goodbyes.

*

I feel my body
burn at night,
in the daytime it's reborn breaking the ashes of my ash.

*

Your flute doesn't play
and the world hushes
among wells and ruins.

*

I saw myself in the eyes of a cow.

*

In the rain
I listen to the flute
and hide behind Time.

*

It's sad, the spring in Ciociara
without the cuckoo's song.

*

Red with blood
the wild berries in the Canterno woods
in October

*

Autumn you take from me
the cuckoo
and the flute.

*

Maybe I recall
the words of my ex-dictator:
"Grass we'll eat, principles we won't trample."

What did grass have to do with it?
"We'll trample men, not principles."
Why is your flute silent?

*

There, in what remains of my village,
autumn is the season of weddings
and of split pomegranates
like the first night.

*

I gather these flowers
that no one is waiting for.

*

In the rushing river we quench our thirst,
I
and a smitten dove.

*

My orphan voice
in the shadow
of the flute.

*

Years have passed since I heard
the flute of my friends
from the other coast.

*

By night
they pierce my flesh
the thorns of Darsìa.

*

I recall the puppies
buried alive by my neighbors
the oxen prodded until they bled by my farmers
while they pulled their carts through the winter mud
and I'm ashamed.

*

From the hill to the sea
they'll call to us at dawn
in the language of refugees.

*

Balkans,
don't swear by spilled blood
but by the song of the flute.

*

My country: my body.
Gëzim: my identity.

MOONACHE

I, Gëzim Hajdari,
creation of trembling nocturnal shades,
wandering cursed from the sacred dwellings,
I confess before the gods,
before temples and oblivion.
I confess before the abandoned fields of my country
and the fires of Hell:
I am the mask of my mask
and what I have written are falsehoods,
it was not me
but a shameful madness
locked in a bare room.
I vow to excommunicate my cursed verses
wherever they may be
and I ask forgiveness from the patient readers
I have deceived
with my mud.

May all the lightning in the sky fall upon you
and the rage of demons,
May Cerberus judge your shadowy soul
among the pitiless flames.
You've lost our trust,
your orphan shade will wander the wintry swamps
will roam like an evil spirit,
may you never find peace in the realm of men!
Rains will fall, snows and filth from on high
icy winds will blow on your word
black rivers will erase your name.
We'll cover your footprints step by step with dust and stones
and you will be condemned to oblivion
by your vindictive bloodline!

O false seasons with your blooming broom and the perfume of violets
in the hedges of springtime

where the joyous sparrow follows the cuckoo
wild rose
poppy petals
fallen in the place of the crime,
pathways with the hissing of vipers.
O years lost in the ruins of blackbirds and owls,
terrible dark labyrinths where I wandered
like a mournful monk
for all this time
in the name of a Father who never became man.
O beautiful days
used up in vain
in a castrated country
throwing stones windward
and writing with the knife point in my flesh
songs of love and pain.
O whirlwinds of enchanting dreams
may you continue to kill ungrateful poets
without war, without a drop of blood.
I, shadow of my shadow,
condemned to exile by another exile
I curse the world
and I spit in the face of the cruel, hypocrite god,
I loved only my terror and not the song of man.

But you my dear old mother,
you continue to love me like always
you name my name like you did every evening
in the small, wet, country cottage
on the top of the dark hill
you don't pay attention to what I write.
My head is confused
and my thoughts are poisoned,
and if one dawn I hang myself,
it will be for a virgin whore
life for an exile poet is worth little,
it's death that is valuable.

I've decided to exchange this life
for a squalid poem
but you, pardon your favorite son
who loved the trees
standing tightly together.
My name will return
and it will knock every evening at your door
like a bird seeking refuge from the rain,
like a fragile penitent lover.

May your cursed verb be punished throughout the realm of the living
and may your bitter seed be prevented from taking root
in the land of Adam,
repent of your horrible sin
and may merciful god absolve you!

I have always lived among my counterparts
alone and estranged from them
fascinated by my madness
and by the tender eyes of birds,
celebrating my ashes hidden and revealed
by the light of a frightened moon,
witness of atrocious crimes.
Like a murderer on the run
crossing through regions of snow
in the grim silence I loudly laid claim
to my power.
Laugh, you valley
and hide my panic,
rise, you hill
and cover my terror,
sprout, you gloomy season
and destroy my prophetic dreams.
With the robin in the courtyard
who follows me in the flash of broken ice
I share my torment
in this pale autumn.

No one believes in my joy,
the days for me are stony, closed skies
and the nights orgiastic paradises.
The first I knew during childhood
were the falcons on my hill;
they fed on the larks of the fields
and I was pleased with the cries of the victims,
I wore crowns on my head of blooming broom
and I passed in front of the predators' battles
like a king in triumph.
Whoever did not applaud with me was a coward,
this is who I am,
I adored the smiling faces of the tyrants
and I hated before I loved.
Come forward my cruel loves
bite my innocent flesh
stone my brown eyes;
burn my anguish
until my groans have ceased
and your evil will is done.
What are you waiting for
nail me with my words
until I bleed
whip my body with my verses
hang my red heart on the branches
before the crow of crows
enters in your veins
and drinks your impure blood
to rise again as a monster.

O inconceivable and blasphemous things we hear
in this night of frozen stars
while the first turns towards the East to sing:
you will die far from your dark land
destroyed by pain and by immense exile,
deadly thorns will grow from your ashes.

I am a stranger, passing through,
I regret nothing in your realm of perdition,
I lay claim to a different fate;
I know the secrets of faithless life
like the weapon knows its own crime.
There's no venom that will calm my madness
give me to the Father
before I become
the son of cannibals
in the promised desert.

Stabbed by the faithful,
in the middle of a night
of communion
of betrayal
I show my bleeding wound to people:
Desire for the desired mystery.
From the day I lost Atlantis
I have wandered without a destination
through streets and over seas
holding my obsession in my hands
and moonache,
setting fire to
alphabets
eros
goodbyes.
Save me with your oblivion, time.

I know what it is I do, my god
and I ask for pardon from no one;
I, goatherd,
member of the communist farming ex-cooperative
who once ran after the blood-smeared bulls
and the *xhin*
I don't obey your Orders
I welcome the stake
and these verses as a punishment for eternity.

From

PELIGÒRGA

Peligòrga is a collection that revisits my adolescence during the communist dictatorship of Enver Hoxha. These verses are written *yesterday for today and today for yesterday*. They lay dormant in me for decades, they were "buried" in my skin, like the scars of love, in the way that the ancients buried their loved ones with their own bodies.

[Author's note]

*

I don't know what awaits me
some tomorrow in these plains.
Restless, I walk every day
along the thorny shores of false oracles.

Night. But I sing anyway
pretending nothing's going on.
If something terrible happens to me
I'll let my skin ring in the wind.

I'll leave this farmer's world
without having done anything wrong.
On the hills my flock will wander
in search of wells and creeks.

*

My mother came from the city,
a beautiful maiden of the proletariat.
She married the son of farmers
who owned land.

From that distant marriage
I was born, at night,
in a gloomy year,
while father Stalin lay dying.

They soon forgot
my birth in the country.
The village mourned
day and night.

The breasts of mothers
emptied themselves of their little milk.
Standing before the Secretary of the Party
the farmers cried in desperation:

"I'd rather my son die than Him"
shouted the fathers.
The dogs howled into the depths of night
for the tragedy that had occurred.

Like this I came into the world,
with the frightened blood of a baby
and the wish to die
in place of a dictator.

*

When I grew up my parents wanted me
to go to Cairo
to study the Koran,and
 become a mufti.[17]

"When you come back from Egypt"
my grandfather said
"you'll bless the village and the earth
in the name of Allah."

My grandfather Velì
didn't keep the month of Ramadan,
he belonged to the Bektashì,[18]
followers of Rumi.[19]

But I wanted
to become the mosque's muezzin
to invite the faithful
to arab prayers in the evening.

The muezzins from Egypt
had the most beautiful voices.
I prayed God to let me grow up fast,
so I could meet the Nile's singers.

Hard times came
to the Albanian village.
Young dreams were put out
like dew in the sun.

My grandfather died,
poor and blind;

---

[17] Mufti: Muslim theologian.

[18] Bektashì: a mystical brotherhood in Albania to which the poet belongs by familial tradition.

[19] Jalal al Din Rumi: The greatest sufi mystic of all time (1207–1273).

blacklisted by the Bolsheviks
as a Kulak.[20]

And I became neither
mufti nor muezzin.
But remained for the country
a disciple of the sufis.

---

[20] *Kulak*: Russian word with which the regime of Enver Hoxha designated ex-landowners.

*

Where are you fleeing my childhood
and my classmate from elementary school?
Your father was put in the pillory
as an "enemy" of the class.

September's erotic noons
of broken pomegranates
like blood on the first night
soaked the thirsty ground.

In the village of Hajdaraj –
crows, snakes, and poppies.
Every maiden I admired
said "You don't love me!"

At night on the dusty doors
the police often knocked.
Holding his handcuffs
the hangman walked the streets:

"In the name of the people
you're under arrest…!"
on the street or in fields
the agents' gloomy voice was heard.

Men and animals
lived in anxiety and fear.
"Who knows whose turn will come tomorrow!"
people whispered.

*

How I suffered
in those bitter years
Every day I felt
like a man devastated, lost.

Often I thought of ending it all
under the pomegranate tree's thorns.
I don't know why God saved me –
in order, maybe, to make me suffer.

From my window with its broken glass
the *xhin* came and went at night
and holding embers they followed me,
trying to burn me.

I woke upset
and ran frightened from the house.
How many times my mother
comforted me down by the river.

She asked for help
from the magic women of the place.
But none of them succeeded
in releasing me from the evil eye.

"You will forever be
a nail in my heart!"
Sobbed my Nur,
in the fields with her bare swollen feet.

*

I had just turned ten
that long ago spring,
when they brought us in a line
to the city stadium.

We had to be present
at the hanging of a young man.
That's what they told us that morning
in the country school.

The condemned man was a poet
who wrote verses.
"It's for the good of victories!"
our teachers told us.

The moment we arrived
at the place of the *gjama*,
before our eyes appeared
the gallows with the noose.

As curious children
they made us sit before the hangman,
to see up close the punishment
of an "enemy" of the Cause.

"We must crush the heads
of the enemies of the people"
they repeated again and again
with a megaphone among the people.

My blood froze
when the hangman pulled the rope
extinguishing forever
the sweet gaze of the poet.

When someone among the crowd
covered their eyes with a hand
others urged people
to spit on the face of the one brought to justice.

In the evening we returned to the village
without looking back.
Our faces turned frozen,
dark like mud.

I didn't close an eye that night
blinded by the crime.
A deep abyss had opened
in my dismayed body.

Like an echo it follows me through the years
the voice of the poet,
as he recites his verses
with the noose around his neck.

*

Perhaps one day my trembling body
will no longer be able to bear the day's arc,
it will be mercilessly knocked down
by the stones of my verses.

It is an ancient curse
that has persecuted for centuries
the rhapsodies of my bloodline,
killed by blood vendetta.

I can't know if it will be spring or autumn,
if it will rain, or the cuckoo will call
from the blooming broom,
but certainly it will happen at dawn or dusk

on a day like today,
when my books – melancholy monks –
will bury in silence my corpse
at the top of the dark hill.

*

My father was sixteen years old
when he left the sheep in the pasture.
He joined the Resistance
in the name of a dream.

He crossed mountains, winters,
glaciers, in the north-east of Albania,
in the name of the revolution,
of hope and Liberty.

In war he became sick
with chronic illnesses.
For the rest of his life he remained
crooked and coughing.

In the '50s he studied in Tirana
as an engineer,
he distributed land to farmers
in Lushnje, Përmet and Skrapar…

When his father (my grandfather)
was made a kulak,
the directors of the communist party
decided to fire him immediately.

It was June of 1953,
when the daily communist newspaper,
that hangman of the people, called him
enemy of the people!

From that day forward he has taken to pasture
the cooperative's cows.
At the end of the month he receives from the State
only enough money to buy bread.

Every morning, when he went to the fields
his sack contained, along with lunch
a book for him to read
that his tired Nur had placed there.

Saturdays he'd go into town
to buy another novel,
sick, tired, and bent,
walking three hours on foot.

During the winter nights
he told us ancient sagas.
Around the fireplace, in silence
we listened spellbound.

Often we were moved
by his telling.
In the pale light of the candle
tears sprung to our eyes.

The most aching story
was the tale of *Anna Karenina*.
Outside, on the barren hill it rained
and lightning danced.

Once my mother said to him
while she dried her face
"Enough with these stories Rizà,
the children are crying."

But he never stopped telling us
what he read every day,
while he pastured the cows
under skies of rain and frost.

Every evening we sat
around the fire
waiting impatiently
to hear a new saga.

*
I celebrated ferragosto
gathering wild berries
in Ciociaria's hills.

---

*

Balkan spring –
gardens perfumed
with pinks
and violets;

in my flesh –
signs,
wounds.

You bring green grass
to the valleys,

to my verses
new metaphors

and mercy.

---

*

I want the pages of my books
to be what starts a fire in the cottage
of two cold lovers.

TENDING YOUR VINES

Maiden of Ciociaria,
my sweetness, wild flower from Saturn's hills,
you are a hot-blooded filly who runs over the harvested fields
kicking at the wind
full of feminine rivers and smells,
your skin with its scent of blackberry intoxicates wanderers.
The moment I stroke you, your body quivers,
your pubis opens like a fresh rose,
like the ripe pomegranate of my Darsìa
that, touched by the first drops of autumn rain
burst open and dripped onto the thirsty ground,
take me to your hymns, to your shadowy curves.
The smell of your young luxurious flesh bewitches me
and excites my reed,
your plump breasts push upward
toward my naked skies.

I come from a land of eros
and this is why I quiver with desire;
in my village I was surrounded every instant with moments of love:
black figs on branches that opened and dripped
iris flowers the color of your wound enveloped
my cottage day and night.
The honeyed smell of apricots permeated my little room,
and the red mulberry, the blackberries, the sour cherries
provoked my hand and my lips with their must
as if it were the blood of the first night.

Every morning on the grass of my garden I found red rose petals
that had fallen in the night on the green grass
and I became a maddened bull in the arena;
ripe quinces broke the tiles of the stone cottage in the depths of night,
waking me from erotic dreams.
Oh green grapes like your juicy nipples
filled with milk and with desires

the fresh watermelon stroked by my passing foot that cracked open
    immediately,
as today the wound between your thighs
where your waters flow
and run together with my white waters white like the frost of the valleys
the shores of my wet lips
shape themselves to your ardent woman's belly.
Oh the white snow on the hills that called to my mind the veil
of the bride on her wedding day,
oh the sheet stained with blood from the first night
hanging in the garden for all to see,
jujubes and wild red berries like a rosary around your fawn's neck
and the ploughshare that tilled the land as if it were the ripe body
of my beautiful neighbor back then.
I drink your virginity like a madman
like I drank the juice of the pomegranate
broken open on my hill those October afternoons;
my youth flowed by in torment
my Darsìa provoked my eros every moment, day and night.
What did I not do to placate my sexual instincts in that time
of Albanian dictatorship,
flogging that lower part of mine linked to sin
and drinking goat's milk.
These were the hard times of state chastity,
whoever stole a kiss committed heresy
and ended up in prison for rape and violence,
a strange spectacle of life played out in my country
and it fell to me to be born exactly in the most erotic,
most prohibited region in the world;
where I saw the farm laborers castrate the testicles of the bull with stones
while the young calf watched astonished at the cruel
punishment inflicted on her beloved,
no one has ever seen such a terrible castration.

I want to explore you cell by cell,
I want to drink all the rivers of your lakes that will quench my thirst
all your full moons;

no one can travel over you as I can ex-goatherd,
shout, scream more, more I want to hear each of your deep cries
I'll satisfy every one of your rough desires,
I want to travel over your trembling skin like a knight in triumph
I'll bathe in the pleasure of your golden shell,
the naked hills of your peach-like breasts.
Cry, laugh, go mad, I want to fall
on top of your body like a martyr on the field of battle
faithful to his captain
killed with his own arrow.
Your woman's hunger doesn't scare me
I will enter your arena without weapons and without armor
only with my wild horse,
without saddle, or bridle or cinch.
I'll tame your forest fire,
I'll bathe in the pleasure of your golden shell,
I'll listen to your sounds to your dark and your shadows,
I'll feel your timeless cave vibrate with passion.
I am your wandering bull who hangs on your warm breasts
spring garlands, as once they hung broom flower garlands
on the horns of goats in my native village.
All those who desired you before me are merely unworthy men,
all those who travelled over you before me lied to you.
I want to touch the depths of you, to quench your flame with my flesh,
invade me with your hands like a an enemy who has surrendered,
make me lie on a bed of cannibal stone,
devour me, my longing for love is infinite.
I want to delve into you every day
as once I delved into the dark earth of Darsìa
my dove, I am hard and chaste
I possess you like a warlike *robinjë*
and on my triumphing steed I take you to my king,
devourer of prey.
My confession, I breathe your light body, your shivers,
your sighs, your trembling,
I breathe the nectar of your wild rose
while I seize you like the horse seizes

the filly in heat in the rich field.
I take joy in the fruit of your body,
may I satisfy you until you burst into tears
that are warm like the summer rain;
rest your moon in my farmer's hands
give to my thirsty lips the taste of your tender, ample lips.

Open your white dress,
I want to drink the perfume of your ripe sex
glad to be fertilized by my desirous member;
cover me with your body like a tree,
stroke me with your excited breasts that quiver,
oh, your full thighs!
You are pure and your pubis is in flower,
every pathway brings me to your wound,
intoxicate me with your fragrance
like summer rain penetrates into the fissures of the split earth,
thus I too will penetrate you because I am your monsoon.
I am keeper of your dark, guardian of your fire, tender of your vines,
You have become my first country without tyrants,
a new exile; and I nominate you queen of the exiles in flight
towards the thin line of the burning horizon.

– I'm scared! You are a wanderer and one day you'll leave
you won't keep your promise the besa
and my soul will never again find peace at the top of the dark hill,
you will only make me suffer, you man with falcon eyes,
I won't let myself be transformed into dust and ashes;
but the moment you touch me, I give in
my flesh quivers, I lose my memory
and I surrender to your warlike steed.
My mad lover, arrived from the cold with the cold,
come, I want to make love twelve times a day like a grouse;
I am young and I will satisfy you,
I will intoxicate you with my Oriental perfumes until you lose
your way home, I will guide you from hill to hill,
from fire to fire, from valley to valley
from green to green.

*I'll bring you to my land in the region of earthquakes,
I'll tell you oriental tales of treachery and betrayal,
I'll transform you into a cuckoo that makes its nest in my shadowy woods
and never abandons the place of its singing.
In my bed you will forget your Eastern country
that bore you to be its martyr
and I'll save you from the curse of the* xhin.
*I love you for your nights for your heart of ice,
for your knives sharpened on stone,
for your delirium;
my seed of farmers
I want to be your village goat from time long ago,
so you can drink from my juicy breast
that will increase your desire as a virile ex-goatherd.
I will become your favorite
because I can read your destiny
and call to you with a different alphabet;
I will ask your Zanas*[21] *to teach me how to read
the sky and the earth like your ancestors did,
to bewitch and seduce your soul barren like that of a mournful monk.
I will steal from the brides of the river the key to open the impassible door
of your empty room
and I'll offer you a bittersweet cup grown in the fields
of your wandering verses
and I'll see you at my feet.
I'll suck the bitter flavor of your exiled lips,
I'll kiss you up to the point of death
to subdue you just one time
and be queen
and you the guardian of shadows that are missing from the Kanun* besa.

– Kiss me and have pity on this martyred body
that radiates joy and fear
and wanders from exile to exile,
humiliated and offended by the tyrants of its first country.
Kiss me and pray for these arms that have survived dictatorship

---

[21] *Zana*: alpine demigods according to popular Albanian belief.

and have been wounded in liberty,
for these hands grown in naked rains
for these lips that tremble under the dark sky of the West,
for this Verb that has become love and sacrifice.
Gather in these beaten, bloody eyes that have fled the death of night,
always alert thinking that someone follows me;
bless this gaze buried by Time,
take these black thorns from my skin,
soothe my stigmata,
caress my stones
to lighten their weight before they kill me.
Don't you hear the red blood that pulses in our veins,
the *peligorga* who sing in our fingers?
My grouse with your Oriental perfumes,
let us love each other as we face the knives
and in the dawn we'll be reborn again in this world of terror;
let us kiss each other's innocent bodies, condemned to the border
as if it were the last kiss of the last day,
as if it were eternal,
to try, if possible, to love each other one more time.
Don't be scared, it's the frightened turtle doves lifting up in flight
and the shadows of the hills that fall on our bodies,
now lightning dwells in the sea caves beyond the profane eye of the day.

– I don't know whether to bless or curse the day I met you,
your love:
joy or misfortune?
my wandering passer-by
fill me with yourself
and let your bull travel my fields
and my white dunes.
Let your raging devil quench itself in my springs,
I am burning, cross over me with your xhin,
with your Zana
with your oracles,
with your stones.
Plant me with seed, fertilize me,

bite me as you bit the blackberries,
touch me as you touched the sour cherries,
suck me as you sucked the split pomegranates of your hill,
flood me with the white foam of your full river,
flood my valley of red poppies
and make your fertile god lose himself in my dark moon!

From

DELTA OF YOUR RIVER

*

I am going away Europe, you old foul whore.

Your ruins no longer enchant me
your mirrors and your abysses
have misled my exile,
wounded my mournful Eastern body
in front of these false petrified altars.

Goodbye Europe with your walls,
your drowned voices and your graves
made of water.

My castrated country compelled me to leave,
your eunuch saints abandoned me in the rain, like a stranger.

Tomorrow, early,
I'll leave with the first boat on the Tyrrhenian
from the port of Circe
accompanied by the fatal songs of the Sirens,
towards the Southern Cross
without turning around.

In the distant deserts
unknown wanderers await me
warriors of ancient tribes, belly dancers;
I'll steal maidens from the courts of the kings of borderlands
just like *Halil* [22] of *Jutbina* [23] of the *Bjeshkëve të Nëmuna*,
so I can give them as brides to my leader, and give life to a new bloodline.

---

[22] *Halil*: a legendary character of the Albanian Epics.
[23] *Jutbina*: Borderlands between Albania and ex-Yugoslavia.

I'll burn the old, rusty languages
I'll shake identity off my back – citizenship and motherland, too;
I want to spend my years in prison
far away from my books
with honest outlaws and bandits.

Goodbye Europe with your blood spilled
in the name of assassinating borders and of bloody flags.

Tomorrow, early,
I'll leave with the first boat on the Tyrrhenian
from the port of Circe
accompanied by the fatal songs of the Sirens,
towards the Southern Cross
without turning around.

*

You're a black goddess dipped in the stars of the savanna,
on your journey through time's oblivion.
Silent, you travel over my burning flesh,
like the full moon through the dark
woods of the Congo during the short summer night.

You bring the air of the savanna
in your hands and on your ebony neck
the stars of the Sahara.

Your antelope eyes – birthplace of ocean nights,
your silken skin – perfume of mango,
your heron's body – fruit of passion
that rose out of the bowels of the red earth
like the night of destiny.

An erotic wind blows from the Indies
and lingers over our burnt forests.

Who will show us the path
to return from the equator?

At night the ruthless waves
bite the white sand of the riverbank, you

tremble.

*

I danced with the Masai on the crater of Ngorongoro
called volcano and Olympus of the black gods
in an afternoon of rain and sunshine
dressed in bright red clothing
and armed with lance and a big stick
the symbol of strength and protection.

I prayed with the young, firm-breasted virgins
for the light spirits of the dead
who dwell in the dark forests,
and for the love of the savanna
prayers in an unknown tribal language.

I leapt up in the high jumps
of the ancient tribal rite
and I saw the *morrani* [24] feeding
on hot zebra blood
sucked from the neck of the living beast and drunk through a straw
together with white milk.

I spoke with the warrior shepherds
along the muddy reed-filled rivers.
The manes of lions they killed
they wore on their necks
body to body in the Tanzanian savanna.

Returning to Dar es-Salaam they trusted me with a secret
handed down from their forebears for millennia:
don't whistle in the evening
because it hurts the spirits of the ancestors.

---

[24] *Morrani*: hunters of lion heads, they kill lions in hand-to-hand combat without firearms, they wear on their necks the mane of the animal as a badge of honor.

*

Your naked skin like the dark forest of Ngorongoro,
your eyes the color of Africa like the Indian ocean at dawn,
your full breasts reaching high like black solitary hills
your stomach smooth and fiery like the thirsty savanna
before the rainy season,
your pubis in flames between the high thighs of a gazelle
like a golden shell.

*

Vast evenings of flame like the skin of a wild Sudanese bull
light the red indigenous earth. The line of the equator
burns in silence, black rivers bring with them the suffocated voices
of the secular dark. On the baobab branches birds await nightfall
with songs of distant childhood. The witch doctor consults the king
of the Baganda tribe in front of his royal hut every time he exits and
           enters.
Below, the herds group together under the open sky to ward
off the predators always in ambush. The black pulse of Africa
beats. Little by little the noises of the tribe hush leaving room
for the lunar night and the light spirits who watch over the rivers,
those protectors of the savanna and of the women of the warriors.

*

Where do these bloody men go now they've reached the dawn?
Their eyes are barred with terror.
They say they come from the Delta
of Niger and they don't want to turn back.

What will become of their destiny?

They flee along the border
together with maddened beasts
defenseless against unknown dwellings
and the voices of the dead.

*

All the way out here in Ciociaria
your young filly's eyes, raised on the fruit of the acacia, reach me.
Your eyes: indigenous earth without trees without shadows
they cross the African nights with the night.
Your eyes: windows where only sand blows.

*

The blind night on the walls of Arusha
wraps us in darkness like a dog's hide,
it closes the pathways of light that return to the homeland.

We surrendered to its arrows of love;
we didn't throw stones or drops of venom.

The thin line of cries separates us from the savanna,
from Kenya the snowy summit of Kilimanjaro
like the truth of a grey-haired dream
captured in the memory of the baobab.

We speak of an Africa drunk on its blackness
not far from the plantations of coffee
and the herds of the Masai divided by felines.

At the elevation of your lips
gold and blood the night of Arusha.

*

I crossed the Sahara
quenching my thirst in the oasis of your eyes

To the sand I gave my memory
and to oblivion my verses.

Where does this infinite nakedness lead me?

Toward the dawn the Tuareg people of Taudenni
will go beyond our names.

*

On the dusty streets of Bamako
among the *peul*[25] and the warriors of the Sahara
who pray in the mosques of Djenné.

In the colored stalls of Bamakò
among the noises and cries in French and in *bambara*
of the fishermen of the Niger river.

In the immense bazaar of Bamako
among the masks of the Dogon and the calls of the muezzin
and the desert-like voice of Ali Farka Touré.

In the erotic, serpentine streets of Bamako
among the swords and knives of the Tuareg people
returned from the salt mines of the Taudenni.

In the chaotic imperial city Mandinga
among the voodoo rites and the beautiful women of Timbuktu
who show the passerby one single eye.

*

The women of Ségou do their washing on the banks of the Niger river
they smack their clothes on the rocks and sing in *bambara* lullabies of love
for their Tuareg men. They do not stop watching the eyes of the crocodiles
that approach children on the bank. The sun burns.
The waters of the Niger, dark and cloudy for centuries
flow bloody towards the burning south
bringing sad glances from the faces that cry out to the sky.
The wind of Harmattan takes off their clothes, makes them appear nude.
Voices get lost. The women of Segou do their washing in the Niger river
and they spread the clothes over the rocks. They sing in *bambara* lullabies
      of love
for their Tuareg men, with their black breasts bared to the wind.

---

[25] *Peul*: shepherds of the savannahs of Mali.

*

The young *cheleb* with their muscled bodies painted
go maiden-hunting along the valley of the Omo.

"O women if the *Surma* tribe with your cheeks like pomegranates,
come with us into the green forest;
we'll feed you with acacia fruit and with the dates of the desert oasis
come in the evening with the rains."

"O young *cheleb* so full of desire we cannot abandon our people –
far from our huts we'll die of sadness."

"O delights of the *Surma* tribe with your braids
we'll make new huts for you and we'll found a new bloodline!"

O young *cheleb* lovers, we'll wait until night falls
to come to you in the green forest.

The desire to feel your skin makes us burn.
We'll come to your tents in the dusk,
we'll give you our breasts the color of camel's milk to drink from.

We'll sleep with you in the green forests of the southern valleys
we'll love each other on the white stones of the rivers
surrendering to your muscular arc in the hour of pleasure."

*

I arrived at Cairo by night from the desert of the north,
the dark of the Aegean and the fatal songs of the Sirens.
I fear I might disturb the eternal sleep of the pharaohs of Giza.
What a long voyage to this city of the phoenix and the arab bazaar.
The city of Tutankhamen sleeps at the feet of the Sphinx
like an encampment before battle. The full moon on the Nile spies on us
through the bare branches of the date palms. Carts full of grain
leave for Rome. At the port of Alexandria where once Ptolemy stepped down
in his flight from Athens, I am welcomed by Mohamed Ali Pasha,[26]
grey-haired with his advisors. The sweet air of the royal court
leads me among young slaves and eunuchs. Powdered pomegranate seeds,
vanilla from Zanzibar, and honey from Oman are offered to guests.
After the banquets and the maidservant belly dances, into the bed of Cesar,
redolent with balsam and incense, the unfaithful Cleopatra leads me.

*

Equatorial night. Tam-tam. Stars, darkness and distant childhood.
From the bush come the mysterious songs of the night birds.
Sounds, rhythms, and verses of Okot p'Bitek penetrate my Eastern skin.
Never have I been so far from my country and my cannibal stones
the place they would rather I die than live. I breathe the black air
sweet like honey from the flowering date palm. I listen to the beating
of the red earth, the rites of the witch doctor and the ancient voice of the
      living.
Early tomorrow under the trembling curves of the new day,
ebony hands will offer me passionfruit.

---

[26] Muhammad Ali Pasha (1769–1849): An Albanian military general and wālī of Egypt starting in 1805.

*

Vultures and black clouds in the sky of Uganda.
"When it thunders at the equator, it rains on the Congo" says Zaira,
a maiden of the *Peul* tribe, the shepherds of the savanna.
Lying on the grass I drink the light of falling stars.
No regret for the country of the East, in my veins
it has planted only panic and terror. In those native hills
are hidden the ashes of my green years. Alas, my friends,
valleys of partridges and falcons, may you be blessed. Inside me
burn the fires of the northern savanna.

*

It's big, Uganda's moon. Hung from the thin line of the equator,
it illuminates my flight from a country that nourishes to kill.
The hungry felines sense the smell of blood and go looking for prey.
Suddenly the sky closes over with low clouds as dense and dark
as the skin of a zebu. It lightnings over Burundi. Ancient calls from the
        forest.
The star of Thompson illuminates the little streets of the indigenous village.
It's the heart of night, the tribe prepares with songs and dances.
Tomorrow is the festival of the virgins and the prayers
that will help the trees to grow beautiful flowers filled
with nectar for the bees of the forest.

KEEPING MY VINES

Falcon Man who comes from the stony earth of Darsìa,
fled from your country in the spring
by night, in the rain,
defeated
without a handshake
listen to my maiden's call:
don't abandon my unripe vine
I am young, I still want you
your winters
your rains
your foreign shadow.

My filly's body trembles
come tame the blaze,
the flames invade my fiery belly,
my skin dances
my veins sing
my breasts tremble
my red lips burn,
the dark moon of my sex
sprouts flowers of eros.

Forget your bitter exile
your Eastern motherland
beyond the black sea,
the two-headed black eagle that devours without mercy
your weak flesh
as passersby watch.

In your Balkans
delirium and dust,
no one is waiting for you
except the curse of the *xhin*;

I want to soothe the wounds the stones left on your body
and the punctures black thorns made in your skin
with the pure must of my grapes.
Don't fear bad spirits,
no man is knocking at your old door,
no one is following you to stab you.
There is time before your books – those mournful monks –
bury in silence your corpse
on the bare hilltop.

Give yourself to my longing for love with your *xhin*
your stigmata,
gather up my woman's call
in this trembling peninsula of drowning black bodies.
The gods made you descend from the alps of Arbëria
to put you to the test of love
to proclaim you equal to them
to meet me, maiden,
come to Ciociaria from the seas of the south,
messenger from the exiles in flight.
Your Albania, mother and gorgon,
bore you and grew you in order
to devour you among the stones
cursing your body
your tongue
your eyes
until you were blind.
Don't turn back to look at the Balkan country,
in your skin only black thorns and deep stigmata,
at the summit of your native hills lies the terror of the *green years*.

Exiled Man
I am your vine in the reign of Earth
I come from the bowels of the red dirt of Saturn,
to make you drunk on my maiden's nectar
so you'll lose the path back to your Darsìa,
to make you die and be reborn a thousand times in exile.

I want to be prisoner of your savage destiny,
like the field watered by the rains of autumn,
I want to be the hymn of your flexible reed.

You are the drop that nourishes me in exile,
you wet me like rain wets the broken earth in autumn,
you keep me awake, alive in the peninsula of earthquakes
you fertilize me from season to season with the full moon
and you close my circle.
I want to breathe my exile through your skin.

Man of farms and countryside,
I want to be impregnated in your old fashioned village
on the dark hilltop, green with grass for grazing,
where the blood-smeared bulls vie against each other in the
        harvested fields
and the lightning is born.
I want to give birth to a new bloodline
so that your warrior's struggle may continue
so your name carved into the stones may persist through the centuries
and so your Word will reign in the realm of Men.

Kiss my full lips,
bite my nipples like you bit the red fruits
of the *razaki* in Hajdaraj,
kiss my breasts like peaches on the hills of your village,
sweet like *halwa* from your East,
like the *pekmez* of the red mulberry that Nur prepared for you.

Taste the succulent fruit of my valley whose scent is like the musk of the
        linden tree in the woods of Çapok,
and gather into your bed of flint my night-shell.
Cover my body that yields to your mystery,
drink my fawn's neck,
grasp my graces in your prophet's hands,
name my fingers for branches of springtime.

Laocoontian Man,
enter my thirsty forest with your thunder
and the lightning from your farming lands,
quench my thirst in your spring.

I am the clean grapes of September
that hang into the courtyard of your wandering Word,
and you, exile and caretaker of my vine.
My arms: branches that sanctify you,
my hands: ropes that bind me to your hands,
my fingers: roots that wait to dig into your ripe body,
once a goatherd.

Your exiled love
your stranger on a journey love
your heretic love
your blasphemous fertility love.

Bull Man perfumed with eros,
when you look at me I become wet
when you caress me, I become woman
when you possess me, I surrender to your *xhin*.
When you touch me in my depths, I cry out,
when you dig into me with your plowshare, I weep with joy,
when you empty yourself into me, I feel your erotic energy
cover my naked skin
like the breath of wind that caresses the waves
of a desert dune.
I am your dune,
your flight,
when you die in me, I am reborn in you.

Balkan Man,
I am your *robinjë*,[27]
I want to be bought by you at the flower market.

---

[27] Robinjë: A maiden who was taken alive from the winning warriors and given to the masters of the war as a trophy.

My body is a disarmed soldier
ready to be pierced by your innocent sword.
Let your white rain fall on my black forest
and break the banks of my waters.
I want to shout to the world that I desire you,
I want to confess to the world that I love a man,
I want to cry out to the world that you are man
and I am woman.
I want to stop people on the street and say:
"I know that you don't care but I love an epic man!"

Warrior Man of the East
seize me with your muscular body
like a wild bull of Shegas,
shake me like the spring wind
shakes the buds of the Judas Tree in the bare woods,
make me green with your warm,
as the oasis in the middle of the desert sands is made green.
And make my shell surge with the fruits of eros
in your image.
I love you as if I were celebrating a divine cult in Darsìa,
I sanctify you like the ancient gods were sanctified
in old Arbëria,
I am the priestess of your Temple,
guardian of its eternal flame.

Ulysses,
I am your Siren,
I'll make the journey long
I will wrap you in blind fogs
and I will accompany you with sea shanties,
I'll lead you by way of the unknown ports in *mare nostrum*
to your homecoming in Ithaca
and you will always recall your Arbëria.

DELTA OF YOUR RIVER

My Ulysses,
it is the twenty-second winter that you navigate the dark seas of exile,
surrounded by the fatal songs of the Sirens,
far from the disfigured cities of your Albania
that devour their own children like Medea,
surrounded by loss, pain, hunger and loneliness.

You are the valiant hero that bears the atrocious history of a country
that adores tyrants and beheaders,
condemned to silence by the poets of the court of Tirana,
chased from the country of the black eagles with two heads
one April day
while in your Darsìa the Judas Trees bloomed
and the violets perfumed the air.

It is you who wrote *Epicedio,* the *gjama* of your people,
the woeful destiny that befell its *shqiptar* its men of *besa*;
the gods brought about your birth so you could sing of your *malsor*
        bloodline
stabbed in the back in their own house.
Now your exile's life trembles under the long arc of exile
in unknown cities
pursued everywhere by the curse of the *xhin*.

My lute player with your crow eyes
you come from a bloody and severe bloodline,
you are the last *aedo* of the *Bjeshkët e Nëmuna*.
You grew up in the place where Caesar and Pompey vied with each other,
on the coast of the sea of *Arbëria*,
now prisoner of your heresy in the black earth.
Destiny has always wanted to test you
like it tested the heroes
in the time of Ulysses.

My mournful monk, you live like a warrior
who comes to rest along the coasts of black bodies, drowned, nameless.
Your whole life you've endured the waves of a strange fate,
far from the rocky coast of Ithaca,
drinking the hemlock of exile.

Your body still bleeds from the black thorns
that pierce your stigmata.
My prophet, buried alive in your motherland
by your feline verses,
your eyes and your beard give off the scent of epic poetry,
in your nostrils are the smells of the countryside.
And I nominate you king of the cruel destiny
that tossed you from shore to shore,
from storm to storm,
from sea to sea,
until you made landfall at me, your *shqiptar* Penelope,
your eternal wife from the south given as a gift
to the barbarians *by the Greeks.*

I am your slave,
remember? You bought me at the ancient port of Orikum
from a boat that came from Piraeus.
I am a survivor of the Amazons
that the Greeks sold to their enemy neighbors
in the prison camps of war.

And no one has ever loved you like I do,
Poet Warrior Man,
because no woman, no maiden, ever succeeded in understanding
the mystery of your Word
and the secrets of your manhood.
Water me with the essence of your *luftëtar* manhood,
I will bloom for you with flowers more perfumed than earthly gardens
so I can make you drunk with my pure girl's nectar.

I am your wife and your disciple, and you are my god
of the Cursed Mountains, raised in the shadow of the *Kanun*.
Your name is carved into the stones and tempered on my skin,
your Word written with blood in my veins,
and you, wait for me in the Temple on Saturn's earth.

My sanctity,
last *luftëtar* of ancient Arbëria,
I will bring you as a gift the love of a woman
so I can stand beside you in the fight against the false oracles
and the fatal Sirens on the seas of exile.
I want you to marry me at Darsìa's lake
so the lake can watch over our promises.
As witnesses we'll have Nur, the cow,
and your little donkey of long ago.
And with the pledge of the kiss I'll kiss you on your warrior's neck.

My sacred Gëzim,
once goatherd of the Balkan lands,
I am the delta of your river that flows through snowy valleys,
and you, my altar deconsecrated by the new century.
Your lean body like the body
of a slave at the pyramid of Cheops,
You travel over me like a wild bull in the harvested fields.

My maker,
I am your creation
I let myself be guided by the destiny
predicted by the *Ore* of the *Bjeshkëve*:
that a manly poet like you should have his maiden,
should care for the arrows of his Word,
for battle, and for his steed.
I am your priestess and I will forever keep
the flame of your Temple lit.
I will lead you toward my flaming vine
like the light that leads the day towards the mystery of dusk.

My last epic man
you are the caretaker of these grapes of mine that drip with longing
in the courtyard of your Word.
Do not be saddened by your mournful exile,
the ancient prophecy is being fulfilled:
you will return to your Alps from the "barbarous" lands
climbing down through the mountain passes of the borderlands
as conqueror and liberator,
the crows and the Furies wheeling overhead
while below spread out on the earth are monsters and corpses.

Come down with lofty step from your alpine passes
in the Cursed Mountains
like an ancient conquistador,
like Hannibal crossing the Italian Alps
in order to conquer Rome.
You will not wear on your head the mask of the goat
worn long ago by the captains of Arbëria.
On your shoulders le *Zane*, le *Ore* e i *Xhin*,
in your hands the shqiptar *besa* e the lute of the *malsor*.

You will reach your martyr's Ithaca,
but the gods want to make you wander
along the tempestuous seas,
accompanied by the loneliness of exile, until you

My falcon protector
you'll return to our bed of flint,
and I, your Penelope, will recognize you from the stigmata in your skin
and from the arrows of nostalgia that pierce your Word.
Give me the *besa* that will bring me, one day, on a white horse
to the Bjeshkët e Nëmuna of your Darsìa.

From

INSIDE ME GROWS A FOREIGN MAN

*

I am a poet banished to the heart of Europe,
Europe, that happy cannibal. White-blooded.
The one stroke of luck for this proud man?
I spoke truth in a season of deceit
in an imprisoned country, without true names for its faces,
words of fire on my tongue. Over the curved regions of the world,
behind the thirst of pyres, the tortuous blaspheming streets,
a little of my prophetic life survives, a little of distant utopias,
in secret the swollen cries of rage grow under the skin.
It trembles, this destiny that shattered on stones, twenty-seven years at
    the border
doesn't move anyone. No sign from that other wild coast
that it will go beyond my burned childhood, the mountain of my books
    waiting.

*

Why did you cause me to be born Albanian, blind, and without memory?

I was born from the wound of your womb one Balkan night,
on the dark hilltop, born to see torments and pain
and end my days in shame. At the border, alongside thirsty destinies

Condemned from exile to exile,
far from the land of crimes. Fires, gunshots, clay, and blood inside me.
With the point of the knife on my trembling skin I write
songs of love and pain. Everything becomes sound, gesture, gold.

I flee like an assassin towards the regions of the North
with horror in my hands. What stranger god has carved our luminous time?
Humiliated before they arrive on earth, the living, the dead.

Cursed are the children who drank the milk of your woman's
breast. You didn't bear men, but worms who suck your marrow,
They rape your remains with stones. Why wait for the end to return
to the south and bury my name? In what country?

I weep for your martyred body on the overhanging cliffs
of Ciociaria. Alas! Below, maddened faces float in the mud
under the void of the sky. Voices of false oracles call out from the dark veins
of a sterile land. At the horizon, visions of white temples, distant childhood,
snake venom.

Land stabbed in the back
knifed in the front under the profane eyes of the day.

I dig down into the eternal roots of time so I won't die.

I was born from the wound of your womb one night in February
on the dark hilltop,
born to see torments and pain
and end my days in shame. Fleeing from fire to fire.
Condemned from exile to exile,
far from the cities blinded by stones.

*

My twenty-seventh year in exile. A nail that bleeds. When will it end?
Time slips between my fingers like voices we love lost in the abyss
of the I, the years pierce my flesh like knives. Unknown fires,
the same assassin borders, deadly worries. I don't have the courage to say
      goodbye.

Rivers of letters, floods of verses grow out of the stigmata in my trembling
      body
without rest like black thorns. I have seen so many men die on the threshold
of day without a last goodbye; on their lips, echoes of war, unsaid words,
hymns of hills, fertile ashes. At the top of the world a door covered in moss.

The blackbirds eat the last berries of the elder tree in the hedge in front
of the bay window. Their beaks hold the wounds of the woods. They court
      in couples,
they look me straight in the eye as they jump on the bare limbs of the
      Judas Tree.
Crows and cold slabs of stone make up the season. Nothing promising.

Beyond the Lepini Mountains, in the heart of the Tyrrhenian, lightning
      grows old.
The streets of return to the Balkans catch fire. Bombed cities lie on top of
      burning
books, newly erected walls, escapes and thirsty swords. Delirium and
      madness.

I close my eyes and listen to myself.
In what language will death call to me
in my bare room? What death?

Gunshots from tortoise hunters cross this province stained with red.
Cypress Street,[28] where I live like a poisonous snake, makes its tired climb
up to the Ciociarian hill where the trees stand tight next together.

---

[28] Cypress Street: the author's address in Frosinone, Italy

I am nostalgic for walking with my hands in my pockets in the city of
    Lushnje.
When I went to middle school and high school I sold the milk from my
    goats
in its neighborhoods before going to class.

I returned to the village two hours on foot, in the afternoons
I went to work in the fields to buy our daily bread,
and books for study. The closed sky on my shoulders.

These were the years of terror for the State. Condemnations, death by rifle,
    forced labor
in the name of class warfare. Marches, slogans, barbed wire.

The Tyrrhenian Sea brings through the throats of mountains the deadly song
of the Circe the sorceress,
the hoarse voices of exhausted fishermen,
the nostalgia of those who leave.

*

People see me walking the streets of Ciociaria
and they ask:
"Mr. Hajdari, do you work?"
"Yes – I respond – I am a poet (forbidden word), I work with words."

Last Saturday at the baker's, I met some acquaintances
I hadn't seen in quite some time,
they greet me cordially. They ask:
"My dear, how is your work?"
"Not too bad, I just try to keep going" I say courteously.

Once a journalist from an Italian newspaper
came down from Milan to visit me on Cypress Street
he wrote on the national culture page
"Sometimes a poet lives even in Frosinone!"

Yesterday in the little cafe next door by chance I ran into
a colleague I met in Paris
presenting one of my books.
When he saw me he was shocked. He said:
"Gëzim, what are you doing here?"

This morning in front of the Academy of Fine Arts
I was stopped by a refugee of color asking in halting Italian
"Friend, give me money!"

I responded to him "Sir, I live hand to mouth, twenty five years in Italy
I don't know what a monthly stipend is."

"You've got money you son of a bitch!" he insulted me, enraged,
following me with a menacing face.

My old friends from Frosinone
strangely don't say hello anymore.

Inside me grows a foreign man.

*

The wife of my Albanian friend Tefik
ran off with her lover
to Northern Italy.

My friend who works as a laborer is desperate, drinks and sleeps
on the benches of the train station,
hoping in vain that his woman will return.

On his back his yellow summer shirt
in the middle of winter.

*

You, my dear old mother, you have closed yourself into your stone cottage
on the dark hilltop in Darsìa. You've shrunk.
You have trouble seeing. Your light steps in the courtyard
covered with mallow weed don't frighten the blackbird or the magpie
        anymore.
Lunch and dinner you eat cornbread and yogurt.
You cover your head with the same scarf that I bought you
twenty years ago in the American market of Ciociaria.

Lightning and thunder light up your old bed
in the corner of the little room. I don't know if you shut
the windows and worn out door tightly. Perhaps now you are
praying the evening prayer, asking God
to give your son good fortune in life. Peace be with you.

On sunny days you lean on the ledge. Silent.
The black line of the wild geese aims toward the lake
of the region. You know the cry they make at dusk by heart.
No one calls your name in the street as they once did.
In the abandoned village almost no one is left.
at night the wind whistles and the copper moon spies among the olives.

Do you remember when we lived together? I was eight years old.
I got up early to take our little flock of goats
to pasture, then I went to elementary school in the village.

How can I forget the infinite waits in front of the district prison
of our city to see your husband and my father locked up because he was
        the son
of kulak. We returned bitterly to the village without having seen him.

At dusk you returned from the fields of the communist cooperative,
you worked shoeless winter and summer for a piece of bread.
In the evening, tired and worn, you begged me to pluck the black thorns
from your bleeding feet with a needle.

When I lost a goat in the pasture my father bit
my head off, I spent the night hidden in the wheat. You, crying,
your voice feeble, called to me from the streets of the village
until late into the night.

Alone in the dark Balkan nights. Outside the fox's cry
and the barking of our dog. You can't manage to sleep a wink.
You think "Who knows if Gëzim is cold or if he has anything to eat!"

*

His menacing voice every morning early
when I took the little flock of goats out,
before going to school,
to the bare hilltop
with the starlings and swallows arrived from Libya.

"*Haràm*,[29] you have to be the best in your class,
otherwise you'll have to come work the land
you can't live on my labor!"

I grabbed my backpack full of books hanging from the nail behind the door
I ran to school dodging lightning and thunder.
I wore rubber shoes filled with holes, my feet wrapped in plastic bags,
in the rain I recited from memory the day's poem.

I wore my big brother's old jacket with the sleeves
taken in. My bowl-cut hair done by our neighbor's
sheep shears. In class I sat in the front so I could hear
every word of our teacher Christina who came from the city.

In the evening he came home soaked with rain from head to foot, spared
by the lightning. In his pocket a wet and muddy copy of *War and Peace*.
          His mouth
open, big hands, two eyes carved into his face. As cold
as an ice statue he ranted against the dictator.

"Quiet! They'll hang you, you'll ruin the our children's life!" –
my frightened mother begged him. And we, the five scared children
looked him in the face without daring to say a thing.

After supper he gave the sign for us to sit around the fireplace,
We listened to the new tale that he had read in his brief pauses from work

---

[29] Haràm: word of Arabic origin, in the province of Darsìa, where the author was born, it is used in the sense of "little devil."

in the fields. The cough he picked up in the war interrupted the story
      from time to time,
the story of Russian deeds told in the winter of the Albanian dictatorship.

NAILS OF EXILE

My bloodline of rhapsodes dies on Friday.
Friday the ancient romans executed those condemned to death.
Friday Jesus Christ also died, crucified in the place of a murderer.

My father Riza called to my mother one Friday morning
and told her:
"Today I'll die!
Call Agìm, I want to say my last goodbye!" This is the custom in Darsìa.
Agìm is my oldest brother.

At the point of death he added:
"I'm about to die, amanèt[30] your mother Nur,
sick and without a pension;
the damp cottage roof leaks when it rains;
amanèt Gëzim in exile, alone and far away,
over the black see in Europe, that old vice-ridden whore!"

Then looking out the open window he added:
"Wash my body with fresh water from the well in the shade of the
    mulberry tree,
and bury me in the tomb of my mother, Kadife,
she died a young wife, leaving me an orphan at six months.
I leave this pen of Elder wood as a keepsake
for your brother
who chose the path of poet,
cursed path."

He asked Agìm for his *besa* to pay our debt to the neighborhood
baker, he said goodbye to Nur
and he expired.

It was the pen that I used to write the diary of my life
during the years of terror, of class warfare,
when I came back from the countryside, cowherd,

---

[30] Amanèt: a last word or last wish.

my mother tore it from me afraid it would taken by the secret police.
With the pages of his diary she lit fires to warm us,
five children around the hearth those cold winter nights
in the cottage built of flint on the dark hilltop, in Darsìa.

Riza was the scribe of the village, Sundays
he wrote letters for the sons of farmers who were away at military service.

When they confiscated our family goods during communism,
we were born and raised in little half-buried houses, damp and cold,
poverty never left us.

Friday is the day my paternal grandfather Velì died,
representative of the *bektashi* in our province.
His ancestors came from *Bjeshkët e Nëmuna*
they came to Darsìa because of a vendetta
foreseen by the *Kanun* of the mountains.

Velì married his second wife Zyrà,
a healer of snakebite
much younger than he was
She called her husband "my master!"

Zyrà too died on a Friday
on a day of lightning and rain
in front of the Harbor hill.

Friday was the death day of Zybèr, cousin of Velì,
crushed by a willow's trunk on the banks of the Çapok.
I saw this terrible sight with my own eyes,
I was six years old, he often brought me with him,
I cried desperately, begging for help from passersby.

Friday his wife Mynevèr died
a seer and a junoesque woman.
She had almond shaped eyes
and knew how to read the thoughts of the villagers.

Mynevèr was also a shaman, she communicated with *kecka*[31] and *i xhin*.
She undid the spells that xhin put on the villagers
by casting a counterspell under the full moon.

Friday Osman died, the brother of Zyber,
killed by hasmi on his wedding night
in the marriage bed:
hasmi entered into the couple's room from the roof of the house.

That night the family hid what had happened,
the guests celebrated, they drank and danced happily.
The next day Osman's father turned to the guests:
"Illustrious guests, yesterday we celebrated the marriage of my son,
today I would like us to celebrate his funeral!"

Friday Meje died,
Veli's older sister,
she woke in the night, dressed in white, and went to the village stream,
she spoke with the brides of night.

Friday Lidia died, Veli's other sister
married on the other side of seven mountains and seven rivers.
There was bad blood
between her and my grandfather.
It was said that she had trampled the xhin at one in the morning.

Friday saw the death of Sabrì, in the city of Lushnje,
my father's older brother,
condemned to one hundred and one years by the regime of Enver Hoxha
for having fought in the war on the side
of the party of the National Albanian Front.

He asked to be carried to his native village
to see one last time the hill, the olive trees
to kiss the ground of his birth before being thrown into the ditch.

---

[31] *Kecka*: Beautiful dancing brides that appear by night on the banks of rivers.

When he saw the wild hares running among the hedges
the black birds on the curved branches of the olive trees
and the wild grass growing along the wall of the old house
he wept like a child.

Friday Mustafà died, Riza's older brother,
he beat his wife Hurmà in their courtyard
because after giving birth to seven girls
he wanted the birth of a son.

Friday Hysein also died, drunk on grappa, Mustafa's brother,
that day he had fought with my mother
for no reason,
he was hit by a car on the boulevard in the city.

Hakì, too, brother of Hysein and Mustafa, died Friday,
drinking rakì[32] and discussing Roman law.
He hoped the post-communist state would restore
a small part of the goods stolen by the Party of the Proletariat
to our family.

Friday Fatimè also died,
my father's only half sister,
she went mad.

Friday is when I too will die,
crucified hands and feet by the nails of exile
bearing on my back the weight of all the deadly Fridays
of a severe bloodline.

---

[32] Rakì – a traditional Albanian brandy made from twice-distilled grapes.

*

I gather the forgotten fruit that hangs on the trees by the road
in Frosinone, plums, loquats, cherries, pears, and figs.
      I am not ashamed of being poor.

For years no city in Italy has invited me to read my work.
To pay my bills and call you on the other coast
I do manual labor and construction
in the Giardinetti of Rome. I have become bent.
      I thanked the fucking Lord.

Your pension of 4,000 lekë a month in Albania is not enough
to buy bread and one black coffee per day. You wait for me in springtime,
seated on the stone, in front of the rusty gate
at the edge of the little street. I have gathered some money in a piggy bank
to buy the pills you take for your tired heart.

*

You don't know the wounds of the south
the cracked hands of mothers who rise early in the morning
to make their daily bread,
and do their washing on the stones with rainwater.
In their saddened, shrunken eyes memories flow like water,
children play with bullets from the war,
along the dusty streets, among the cactus fruit,
the sad songs of the widows are heard hill to hill,
the calluses of the dispossessed farmers who walk everywhere,
the crazy cries of the cicada in the olive trees, the perfume of the maritime
       pines,
shouts, hot blood on the earth,
the barking of a dog in the abandoned village, deserted cities,
torsos burned from gathering tomatoes in the searing sun,
desperate, violent loves, abandon, goodbyes,
the anonymous tombs of those shipwrecked blacks from Africa along the
       river,
they dreamed of reaching the promised land.

The south is a wound, an eternity, a ripe orange left to rot
on the ground. The south runs in your veins, lives in your blood, it's a curse.
The south is stolen land, thirst that can't be quenched,
nostalgia you can never shake off your back like an old jacket,
it makes you feel like a man,
it makes you die slowly.

You don't know how to breathe the south, the happiness of people who live
       hand to mouth,
you don't know the hiss of the snake in the gaunt mountains, wild berries
       in the autumn
woods, the gallop of horses heard with your ear against the earth.
The south is a sickness, scratched into the skin, a window thrown open
       that listens to the fishermen on the dock.

The south is bitter grass that trembles, hate in love with itself, harvested fields
with blood-smeared bulls; the south is the motherland where I wrote,
       frightened in the in the middle

of the brambles, on the bark of bare trees, along streams, on cliffs, my first
    verses
and spoke with the *xhin*.

The south is change forgotten in a pocket and brought with you wherever
    you go
in the world like a talisman. It's a luxury you can't afford,
a key that can open every human heart. The south is born from pain
God's sin, child of chaos.

*

Running against the wind towards the mountain.
Climbing up among shrubs and Judas Trees in flower
and coming down to the sea,
arms covered with bits of blood

scratched by thorns.
Tasting the bitter grass of the fields
in the desert night,
Putting out fires at their roots

in the flaming stones.
Drinking from the river's mouth with the tongue of lovers
in the shadow of pure desire
at its green feet.

RISE JESUS, TAKE UP YOUR LASH

Once there was a country beyond the Adriatic Sea
called Arbëri
the ancient *shqiptar* bloodline
lawful heir of the Pelasgi
blessed by the *Ore*
protected by the *Zana*
fed by legends
kissed by glory.
Valiant warriors
men of the *besa*
of the *Kanun* of the Mountains,
generous people
proud in their very blood.
They honored guests,
customs, and their god,
bread and oath
salt and heart.
Five hundred years
to the sound of the lute
led by the heroes
Gjeto Basho Muji
Gjergj Elez Alìa.

Guardians of the frontier
of *Bjeshkëve të Nëmuna*,
respectful husbands,
tender fathers.
They never turned their backs
on the fearsome enemy
in defense of their country
their women.
Handsome, strapping,
noble in virtue.
Lord Byron praised them
in *Childe Harold's Pilgrimage*.

Once there was a country beyond the Adriatic Sea
called Arbëri,
the value of a man
was not his wealth
but his honesty.
An excellent farmer
was as good as a prince,
for the servant
as for the king.
Glorious princes
and simple mountain people
refused slavery,
and their true masters
were wise men.
The *shqiptar* arose
even from the tomb
to keep his *besa,*
his word once given.

Once there was a country beyond the Adriatic Sea
called Arbëri:
with the most beautiful greeting in the world:
"T'u ngjat jeta!" [33]
The land of Scanderbeg,
filled with drama,
bones and blood
through history
for the survival of the Albanian bloodline.
Country of rhapsodes
without equal:
lahuta e *çiftelia*
accompanied each passing life
from birth to death.

---

[33] T'u ngjat jeta! "May your life be lengthened!"

Once there was a country beyond the Adriatic Sea
called Arbëri:
honored like a bride
by its founding fathers,
sung of by bards,
illuminated by mystics.
Poets, priests, *bektashi*.
Men of honor
spent their lives
with the pen and the rifle
defending its lands.

Once there was a country beyond the Adriatic sea
called Arbëri:
a country of *burrnija* [34]
an epic people, sovereign
as no other in the Balkans,
they spoke the most ancient language
on the globe,
their women as splendid
as those rays of the sun
the human eye
never sees on this earth
of God's.

Once there was a country beyond the Adriatic Sea
called Arbëri:
country of eagles
celebrated in song through the centuries
by Virgil, Catullus, and Horace.
It lived for millennia
together with neighboring peoples
of all ethnicities
in time of war
in time of peace

---

[34] burrnija – To affirm the honesty and the honor of an Albanian, it is enough to ask the question, *a je burrë?: are you a man?"*

in joy
and in sorrow.

There is a country beyond the Adriatic Sea
called Albania:
never remorseful
for the crimes of communism.
They have governed together
now twenty six years,
"the democratic party"
and the hangmen of class warfare;
they steal together,
destroy together,
do drugs together,
rape together
kill together
celebrate together
flirt together
get drunk together
vomit together
their binges
pigs and sewer rats.

There is a country beyond the Adriatic Sea
called Albania:
a castrated country,
miserable and damned,
with women who are sluts,
cowardly men
deceitful and wicked,
sons who are traffickers
ruthless killers
hired guns.
The new Albania is founded
on criminals, drugs,
corruption, theft,
dirty money

human trafficking
contraband weapons.
Those who speak out
are forced into exile,
condemned to silence
buried alive.

There is a country beyond the Adriatic Sea
called Albania:
with a short memory,
it adores tyrants
yesterday on the piazza of every city
rose the statue of Hoxha the dictator,
today rises the statue of a puppet-mason king,
a crude and bloody thief,
he killed the fathers of the nation
one hundred years ago
and sold Albania
to money lenders.

There is a country beyond the Adriatic Sea
called Albania:
the Colombia of Europe
everywhere there grow
more plants of cannabis
than blades of grass.
Country of scandals
international intrigue.
Corrupt politicians
are elected
by their bosses
as premier
and president of the Republic.

There is a country beyond the Adriatic Sea
called Albania:
thrown into the mud

by dark Powers
from across the Ocean,
with the blessing
of the Mafiosi politicians of Tirana;
sustained by the horde
of pseudo-intellectuals,
journalists,
pundits,
professors,
priests,
muftis,
who suck the blood
 of poor people;
their stipends
stink of crime
and feed on corpses.

There is a country beyond the Adriatic sea
called Albania:
it barks like a dog
at the top of a hill of garbage,
in the shadow of the statue
of George Bush Jr.,
and Hillary Clinton
two bloody
war criminals.

There is a country beyond the Adriatic sea
called Albania:
with poets, writers and artists
corrupt and fucked
from A to Z,
they sold at auction
the country and their mothers.
To obtain their government appointment,
fearful of god
they spit on Allah

they kiss the cross,
they wear on their necks
chains of gold
with the bloody nails
of Jesus Christ.
The poets of Tirana
spiritual prostitutes,
happily sold themselves
to that day's government
at low cost
in exchange for rape
career prizes:
the Pen of Gold
the Pen of Silver
national honor,
publication elsewhere
invitations from Foundations
writing residencies
scholarships
for them and their children
and their lovers.

Awarded prizes by the president of the Republic
the very same day
the very same hour
as the hangman of Enver Hoxha's regime
his "persecuted victim"
of Spaç

There is a country beyond the Adriatic sea
called Arbëri:
where the poets of Tirana
little tyrants,
elected ministers, ambassadors
enjoy from the state
golden stipends
pensions, houses

armchairs in government
on television
in parliament
consultant-slaves
of the heads of the puppet State,
of the thieving Premiers.

There is a country beyond the Adriatic sea
called Albania:
gangrene of the Balkans,
a danger for the continent
Rise Jesus
Take up your lash
Chase the money lenders out of Albania
with whatever it takes
liberate us from the tyrants of Tirana.

*

Marsala,
chalice of the god of deserts
remember man

The arc of time
against the shadow of walls.
you come from destiny's night.

Lilybaeum[35] doesn't see Libya
her eyes sealed by darkness
the drunken thirst of Dido's sea.

Nostalgia for water
in the light of the lighthouse
the dream discovered.

Lilybaeum recalls Libya
it imitates the peace of the stone
from its blue eternity.

---

[35] Lilybaeum: The ancient name of Marsala.

CATANIA

Sea-eye
Etna's ashes
burning lava flows into the Bove valley
an epic wound
still fresh.

ELEGY FOR MY FRIENDS THE EXILED POETS

The fear of dying in another language
in a bare room
without burial
torments the exiles in the West.

My friends the poets left young,
they will die in poverty
loneliness
and desperation.

The Ciociarian poet, Luigi Pacioni
returned from the Black Forest
left for Afghanistan, India, and Kashmir
to burn his body
on the pyre of the dead at Benares
so he could be reborn as incorruptible stone
forged in the flame
unchangeable by war.

Obsessed by the search for the meaning of life,
of love
of death
like Gilgamesh;
in his soul: disquiet, demons, vortices,
maddened swords and marvels.

The *gjama* came at five in the morning.
Summer. On the sands of Sabaudia
on the banks of the Tyrrhenian Sea.
He was twenty-eight years old.
He slept in the shadow of the goddess Kali,
they tied him hand and foot
vipers and hungry reptiles
sea monsters
rose out of his paintings, his strange canvases.

You went out early
running like a crazy person
towards the water of the dark sea,
yelling like a werewolf over his atrocious destiny.
Beaten bull.
Your body
wrapped in a mantle of fire.

What unlucky star struck the joy of your living
what unknown power attacked your life
what divinity cut off your unfinished love?
A sea of blood flowed from that severed love,
the stars blackened,
the moon bled
the sky closed over with stones.

Like a woman who doesn't love us
you separated yourself from the life you did not lead.
Radiant death,
the only bedfellow
who is eternally faithful.

The arc of your life was brief
a passing meteor
the gods loved you very much
the chose you to be their equal,
dove of flame and of pleasure,
wild lily wilted while flowering
you survived yourself.

In your eyes lived the eros of a Hindu maiden
the ashes of the inferno of Benares
the destiny of seers
fixed in a forest of thorns.

A butterfly on your lips sealed your last breath on the shore
in the shadow of the sorceress Circe's mountain.

Heleno Oliveira,[36]
was born in Santa Clara
of the love of a white European man and a black woman,
a braid of ruin and splendor.
The nephew of Afro-Brazilian ex-slaves,
he loved and hated his colonial father.

It weighed on him like a boulder to be this fruit of a black and white love,
descendant of the Zumbi
prince and leader of rebel slaves
who threw themselves off the Alagos cliff
so they wouldn't fall into the hands of the conquistadors
or the hunter of blacks Domingos Jorge Velhos.

His gaze was serious,
his savage rage that of being a man.
Desaparecido,
you suffered so much
loneliness
from exile to exile
singing the lights of desperation,
far from mother Africa,
far from Brazil,
far from your native city, Reice.
Proud of your blackness,
black honor,
the root of the world,
the memory of crime.

Your verses still bleed
ruined blood.
Wanderer in words, seller of stories,
of your story
the point of a knife.

---

[36] Heleno Oliveira (1941–1995): In his early years he was part of the Focolare Movement. In 1962 he became assistant professor of Portuguese literature at the University of Belém do Parà, in Porto Alegre.

Dancer of chaos,
you arrived in Florence one morning in December
shouting from your Hades:
"I am of mixed blood,
will I be received?"

Dear Heleno,
no one is received by anyone,
our boats never reach dry land,
they travel toward ourselves.

In your Florentine exile
your naked soul
was expropriated,
thrown into the street
the way a fired worker
is thrown out of a factory –
some family's father.

Heleno died at fifty-one,
alone.
He was never "received" by the poets of the "high language"
of the "Belpaese" of deceit.

When he felt the end was near
he thought his death wasn't real.

He fled three days to Portugal
and found his Florentine death in Lisbon.

The Iraqi poet and journalist Thea Laitef[37]
died at forty-one.
Sixteen years of exile on the banks of the Tiber,
he found refuge in a damp hole beside the Aurelian wall,
loneliness, ruins, and silence.
Not even the chirp of a bird at his door.

---

[37] Thea Laitef: An Iraqi journalist before his exile.

Seven deserts away from the Tigris
seven oases away from the Euphrates,
camel gone,
tormented in the eternal city.

He arrived in Rome with fresh bloodstains on his clothes,
he was stabbed in the suburbs of Baghdad
by Saddam Hussein's hitmen.

Every day he walked up and down in San Lorenzo
living hand to mouth
always hungry
never a lira in his pocket.
The neighborhood children called him Falcao[38]
because of his long, thick hair.

During those infinite Roman evenings
he sang his nostalgia in the piazzas
on the steps of the Italian capitol he composed his heartbreaking verses.

He dreamed of being buried in Samarra,
next to his ancestors
in the desert
over his tomb a stone
with one verse,
nothing more.

He saw his novel "Far from Baghdad" presented
for the last time in a Roman bookstore.

He expired.
Alone.
In the shadow of the Colosseum.

---

[38] Falcao: P. R. Falcao, a Brazilian soccer player who played for the Roma team in the '80s.

In his hand he clutched an old photo of his poor mother,
next to the lifeless body of this poet
tumbled onto the green grass
the poetry of Eugenio Montale
translated in Arabic.

The waters of the Tiber gave the news of his death
to the seas
oceans
to the deserts
oases
all the way to the Tigris and Euphrates
where his name was written,
where they had been waiting for him for sixteen years
his aged mother waiting
to embrace again her son, now dead.
Your body will be refreshed from afar
by the waterfall of Bikhal.

Italy, mud of your days.

The corpse of the singer of Samarra
remained over a month in the morgue of Rome
because no one could pay the funeral expenses.

The destiny of the poet Egidio Molinas Leiva[39] was tragic,
the son of farmers of Santa Rosa Misiones.
They survived imprisonment
the torture of military juntas,
they spoke the language of their ancestors, Guaraní.

At five he fled to Argentina with his father, a political refugee,
after four years he returned to Paraguay
and lived in secret;
at fourteen he was arrested and tortured

---

[39] Egidio Molinas Leiva: A doctor, a surgeon, and a philosopher.

with his father and older brother by the police of General Stroessner.
At eighteen he was forced to flee again to Argentina.

He organized underground medical services in Southern Buenos Aires
without giving up his political work.
They arrested him again
at two in the afternoon –
five years in the prison of Sierra Chica in Buenos Aires,
eight months of atrocious torture
because he was a member of the Revolutionary Army of the People.
The walls of the cell are stained with your blood.

In August of 1979 he was freed
on condition that he leave Argentina,
he arrived embittered in Rome in August of that same year
abandoned by his wife
who decided not to follow him into Italian exile,
without a farewell
It was a "goodbye."
From across the ocean
silence,
nothing.

The singer of the Guarani language
from a warrior bloodline
survived in Italy by working construction
at Roman sites around the city.
Always solitary and taciturn
with the long arms of a manual laborer
he had the saddest gaze in the world.

I remember the readings dedicated to the Mediterranean those Roman
             evenings.
His colorful shirt hid the plaster stains,
in the hole-ridden pockets of his jacket:
manuscripts
crumbs of bread.
He always wore the same scarf around his neck, winter and summer.

When he learned of his incurable illness
he left to die in Paraguay.
He wanted to be buried in his native village
in the forest of the Amazon
next to the farmers
without land
for whom he fought until the very end.

At the border he was greeted by his ninety-year-old parents
finally able to embrace their son once again
after twenty one years of exile in Europe.
The state authorities did not allow him to enter his motherland
he was forced to turn back, embittered.

He died in Rome.
Alone.
At sixty-four.

The day of his death no obituary appeared in the streets of Rome
at the disappearance of Egidio the bells of the churches did not ring,
there was no prayer to accompany his soul into the beyond
no one followed the corpse of the exile to the cemetery for a final goodbye.
No woman wept next to the lifeless body of the poet.
No newspaper announced his death,
no television program.
No one.

They threw him in a mass grave at Verano
without first or last name.

Hasan Atiya Al Nassar[40]
died in Florence,

---

[40] Hasan Atiya Al Nassar: Awarded a degree in Arab language and literature by the University of Florence.

after an infinite exile of forty years.
Pursued by the poisons of Western cities

thousands of kilometres from his ancient land of two rivers
and the Sumerian night.

He cried out to passersby
that Iraq was the "paradise of the spirit"
but no one responded to his call.
He died saying "Because my beloved Iraq is far away
and I feel nostalgia!"

He fled Nassiria under the waning moon
refusing to fight against Iran
to open fire over the border
killing women and children
old people in prayer
shepherds and camels
muezzins and soldiers.

Destiny brought him to Florence.
"It's a cruel city!"
he whispered to the ghost of Dante Alighieri,
while he walked along the Arno one winter night.

Unemployed. To earn a few cursed lira
the poet of Ur worked as an unofficial attendant
in Florentine parking lots.

God was not kind to you,
he tortured you until your last day
knowing well that you lived only once.

When he arrived in Italy he was twenty.
He passed his exile drinking in bars
the drinks bought by friends.
The venom of alcohol penetrated his veins
and killed him slowly.

"Whoever has not read Ur, Abraham, Gilgamesh, Hasan al Nassar
can't understand what suffering is!"
he would cry in the streets of Florence.

He died at sixty, abandoned
in a hovel without light or heat,
at the head of his old bed
a manuscript like an *amanet*.
In his face:
loneliness
poverty
and immense desperation.

Ancient Babylon weeps for its prophet.

He left without saying goodbye to the woman who gave him
a winter shirt in the summer
the maiden who embroidered the night for him
without closing an eye,
the old woman who gave him a blanket,
his mother who had waited for him for thirty years in Nassiriya.

How could you return to your country
with the flavor of defeat in your eyes
while your Iraq had ceased to exist,
your brothers killed by bombs,
palm trees cut down by weapons' fire,
the library of epic poems of the Sumerians in Baghdad
given over to flames.

Your Iraq devoured,
not even a place to bury the dead.

You walk toward the tent,
the tent for guests,
there is neither rain nor wind,
there is no time

there is wine for everyone
passing through the wounded cities
profaned temples.
They offer you a glass of tea,
the essence of your earth,
fresh vegetables
bread,
virgin maidens.

The fury of death is alone and distant,
beyond the Tower of Babel,
the betrayed disfigured country,
the native land burned
by enemy fire.
The Mediterranean sowed with drowned brothers
scattered over the sea by boats
scattered all over the world,
escaping war.

They'll give you water to drink from the well
and you'll drink with trembling hands
hands born to be kissed
you won't feel alone anymore
with your name
in the ghostly cities of the West.

They won't send you into the fields of battle
the disastrous battle
demanded by the powerful.

You'll walk towards Iraq,
that lost paradise
you'll go beyond oblivion
the weeping of widows
the dead of Ur.

You'll sing like you used to at the breasts of women,
they left sacred signs on your body.
You won't feel like a stranger to yourself anymore
nor to those who loved you,
you'll live all the lives you want
you'll be a child of Adam,
him no.

You return to your country without song,
towards your country of widows
of tombless dead,
towards a poor house
destroyed by human folly.
You return to windows left wide
where sand blows
the echoes of bombing
towards exile.
Forgotten by Iraq.

You'll never see the ruins of ancient Babylon again,
nor the sad dances of the drunken dead
thirsty for a season of peace,
the naked cities
sunk into the heart of hell.
No one will persecute you
with the maddened sword of the Sumerians
you have gone beyond oblivion
and the precious stones of Jerusalem.

Now covered by darkness and ice
beyond the ruins
and the blind violence
under the dark Tuscan earth,
you endured a life that ended early.

I remember Hakim Mohammed Akalay[41]
the ex-president of the National Union of Moroccan Students
a movement that aspired to liberty and democracy
and stood against the authoritarian and corrupt regime of the monarchy.

The berber poet of Tangiers
had Tuareg eyes
a sculpted face the color of sand:
he was a man.
In Italian exile he found no peace.

"I am thirsty for Morocco!"
he told me on the phone.
Premature death
was his salvation.

He dreamed of a free Morocco,
no politicians
no king
with oases
camels
tribes of children.
He carried in his pockets grains of sand from the desert
golden shells from Tangiers.

He painted a picture of his kinfolk every day,
the tomb of his ancestors
the tents of his nomad bloodline
the face of the woman who betrayed him.

He called me often:
"Gëzim, in the stink of exile I've lost my words, my sound!"
He was terrified of being poisoned. By whom?

---

[41] Hakim Mohammed Akalay (1944–2000): Awarded a degree in political sociology by the University of Perugia.

He died when he was only fifty-six,
alone,
unemployed,
in the little Umbrian town of Acquatino Spello
near Perugia

I don't know if they poisoned him,
maybe it was the poison of exile
that cut off his life so soon.

Ali Mumin Ahad
had no country
had no city
fled from Mogadishu
at night, under fire,
in his terrorized eyes
bits of dust,
corpses, laments, flights
black ashes.

Twenty years of exile in Italy,
no work to get ahead
no editor for his books
on the memory of war.
He lived thanks to the help of friends.

He made it out of Rome
before death called to him
from the cupola of St. Peter's.
He fled to Australia
without telling me goodbye.

I'm still alive, resisting between the hills of Ciociaria
and the moors of England.

*

At dawn naked, untraversed streets surround me
unreceived guests wait for sunset to leave
from the right cities, in the right time.

Winter nights won't leave my rainy hands
or my clothing made of light,
the light of the overturned south in the light of the prideless north.

Twenty eight years ago a familiar country drowned inside me,
someone must pray for my innocence
or my damnation.

I saw the gun barrel resting on my temple
ready to do me the favor of exploding my head into the air.
It was 1991: proclaimed by the West "the year of revolution".

I have known what it means to be a man of the *besa*:
the elemental lightness of being in time of war.

*

I turn to you, weak and partial men
of the country of letters,
I won't submit to your sparkling laws,
you know my name well.
You never invited me to read in my home country
or in the grey Albanian diaspora. You lack backbone.
Perhaps sixty two years of waiting are few;
I should wait longer, but without tears
in my eyes, sleepless nights in my hands. Sovereign.
Beyond the borders of the state rain falls on the temples,
the news is garbled, deceives the living,
passing years corrode the simple life.
Why are Kosovo and Albania afraid of Gëzim Hajdari?
They call me "enemy" of the state, strangely, those very men
who were once imprisoned by the dictatorship
under the same accusation.

*

    My poetry: a sovereign country
built stone by stone with effort and agony
by the coarse hands of a farm worker.
It resembles me, clay and blood. Solemn.

    My poetic Europe doesn't take orders from anyone
it's incorruptible, it thinks only of its readers;
it sprouts with the full moon like grafted trees in the countryside,
it's not grown in greenhouses, it feeds on stigmata. Honor code.

    The world of my epics is free,
It doesn't prostitute itself, it lives at the edge of the abyss;
it has the taste of a man from *Bjeshkëve të Nëmuna*,
never lies, tells the truth. It hurts.

    My "heretic" verses, condemned to silence by my country
have no master, they live hand to mouth,
they grow at the periphery of the violent worlds,
nails fixed in the century's forehead. You won't be able to pull them out.

*

They flee towards the north, the west, biblical lines
of men women animals children the elderly walking without a pause
day and night on their feet with whatever fortune gives them
or on boats at the mercy of an unknown destiny white black yellow
hungry in the storms of snow and ice behind them metric tons of ice
        kilometres
of wind the echoes of war and the laments of the dead
the curse of the new century the ancestral calls
goodbyes of separation, walls, borders, realms of the sword
whatever it takes to reach the new world
promised by a lying god.

KAMAL'S LAMENT

I'm frightened of losing my residency permit,
of being repatriated in a country that doesn't exist anymore
a country without trees and without grass,
without wells and without brides,
in a house destroyed by war.
Before leaving Libya
I said goodbye to Kamal, the neighborhood barber,
my teacher of the Koran,
widower, desperate, without work,
his little store burned,
with five children to raise
the orphans of their mother.
He helped me cover with sand,
in the shade of a dry palm,
the bodies of my two parents killed
by the bombs of the West.
He gave me his life savings
to pay for the long trip
to reach Rome.

"Go Abedin, he said to me, here there is no hope
that merciful Allah will protect you,
remember our martyred earth
that gave you life
remember its native houses of dust and ashes
remember your dear kin killed
for no reason,
remember the village where you grew up razed to the ground,
remember the mosque where you prayed.

Don't forget the herds of spiteful camels,
the tent and the glass of tea,
the sacred call of the muezzin
during the hour of prayer
kneeling on the carpet
turned toward Mecca.

Your father worked to raise you
selling dates in the alleyways of Tripoli,
remember the eyes of your mother
before she expired
with your name on her cold lips
the body of beloved Nadira
raped by marines
thrown by the side of the road.

Every night before falling asleep
in the little windowless room,
I think of Libya and I cry.
"Allah why did you spare me?"
Perhaps you want me to go out into the world
to tell the unheard of tragedy
of my slaughtered people.
Far from the desert
bread and water lack flavor,
I lack breath,
I live a half life.
The moment I fall asleep
laid out on an old mattress on the floor
I wake with a start –
I dream they are stealing my residence permit
and turning me over to the police
I'm scared to lose my work
my little rented room
to return to being an illegal immigrant
I am scared I'll be attacked by someone
scared of bleeding out
and being thrown in some canal.
I'm scared day and night
I tremble with fear,
fear of new decrees and new laws
fear of raising my voice
fear of getting sick.
I am scared of the postman who knocks

on the door, scared of the meter reader,
of the noise of my upstairs neighbor,
of the fake refugees.
I am scared of my name,
scared of myself.

*

March 21st the bats fly over the hills of Ciociaria,
April 11th the scops owl gives its cry from the branches of the oak in
 the courtyard,
April 13th the swallows arrive from Lebanon,
April 14th I was forced to leave Albania
from the port of Durazzo, defeated, at night, in the rain,
May 12th I hear the starlings cry as if they had gone mad
May 16th the cuckoo sings on the hills of Ferentino
June 7th the fireflies light the garden next to the *zabel*
July 3 the first cicadas chirp on the trunk
of the maritime pine in front of the bay window,
July 15th every year I gather wild berries at the lake of Canterno
August 2nd I left Italy after twenty-six years for another exile
in the land of barbarians.

*

The sound of bagpipes moves out horizontally before rising up
in fragile balance and moving beyond the thin line of the horizon
where our fixed gazes fall. Perhaps it is a sign of welcome for foreigners,
or perhaps it's an ancient call from the times of Stonehenge
not far from here. Memory hangs between the ports of this rocky, forested
        coast.
Even with eyes closed you can hear when someone walks this untamed
        ground
between the ocean and the edge of the world.

New trees and old rocks study us with wonder,
under our feet roots dig in silence down into the wet earth,
we don't realize that we are already in the strange lands of empire.
For us, people of a savage bloodline, who come from country places
it means that from now on we must live under the sign of obedience
this rule already belongs to past and future history
that given the laws of humanity
no one should escape.
Escape what?

We live like this from generation to generation,
obedience and rectitude. Here it was thus even under the Roman Empire.

To play with fire makes life difficult,
on the island one lives and that's all. It is the destiny of deconsecrated nights.
Those who occupied this home before us
adapted themselves without shedding a drop of blood
they obeyed the sacred alliance in the shadow of the walls.

We've never been so close to the source,
to the true faces we've heard talk of,
to the vortices that kill with maddened swords.
Attentive to the smell of salt on the coarse stones
to the news that turns into noise at high and low tides
unfolding eternal days and seasons.

We seek a temple for morning prayer
a blade of grass to bless our cold words,
a cross to tell the temples about shame
to confess our *gjama*.
On our shoulders the weight of tired cities,
the lullabies of women from the South.

*

To live in bitter enemy lands suspended at the edge of the precipice,
blessed (or cursed?) by an unknown saint. Come from afar,
followed during all this time by the ghosts of other ancestral exiles.

To speak the language of their bloody swords. What flavor
would bread have, or salt or water from the spring for slaves?

Horses' nickering awakens the granite hills of Devon planted with legends
and Roman recollection. The wild hair flees, frightened by unknown voices,
stopping at the plateau's river bank to rest on its hind legs before
running again towards the valley that opens like a lush, green pubis.

Don't give up your names torn out like blades of grass.

Above our heads the copper moon scrutinizes like Polyphemus' eye.
To walk under windy, closed skies that announce new flights
beyond the borders, pushed further to the north where the names
of men and beasts are mixed. A strange slipstream of stony light caresses
        our bodies

Pelican cries pelicans wait for us. Season of roses and knives.
What terrestrial creature sucked the gall from your lips?
Here you'll find only sharp grass, inhospitable plateaus, a list of past lives.
Fig trees don't grow here, nor Mulberry, nor vine, nor pomegranate.

Forget the wild berries of your Mediterranean, forget the songs of the
        starlings
that dug into the mud for their nests as if they had gone mad.
Pastures, cows, and black lines of crows your new home. Without altars.

*

Where do they lead us, these voices we hear, the bells of the sea?
The hills that we trample bring shouts of night inside,
the acrid smell of marine algae after the low tide.
God, if you still exist, there are no other altars on which to pray,
no other crosses for rebirth, nails with which to sanctify oneself.
There are only the cries of rapacious birds above mute heads,
blades of grass that tremble in the cutting ocean wind.
Wet land sprouts mirrors of mud,
beaten horizons collapse onto the spent green,
the pale sun breaks the fragile walls of melancholy mist,
beyond the breathing water, the borders of loneliness, ancient profane nights.

To live perennially at the edge of abyss and oblivion
waiting for the day that will bring the last fires
before crossing the threshold into the dark and eternal void.
We carry in our hands the list of inhospitable places,
new wells grow out of the thirst of our burning memories.
Who in the future will discover these footsteps through the stony arcades,
the signs of foreign loves abandoned in the cold?

Homes that have no gaze, overturned like empty pitchers
in the desconsecrated temple of dervishes.
And us, condemned to perennial silence,
we are persecuted everywhere by the evil speech of power,
from region to region, from border to border.
Woe to whomever denounces the tragedy.
Ever more feeble, the rusty voices, recollections from time before,
echoes from the hiss of the snake return to us in the harvested fields.

Wild animals cut off our paths
vigorous bucks with icy eyes and a challenging air,
they stare at us for a moment, then proceed with the authority of princes
deeper into the nordic forest. A young white male jumped over a crevasse,
lightness and power, followed by the young female in heat.
Drunk with love, trials, and daily dangers
they don't fear the abyss.

*

It's snowing on Dartmoor.
The boulders of Stonehenge,
by persisting with their secret
are emptied of mystery.

On the apple tree
braided roots
pierced by rain's knives.

Water and blood
the tree of Jeremiah.
Rape or passion
this new home?

It's snowing on Dartmoor.
A white shroud over exile.

*

Waiting for the echoing call
that never comes
my metaphors are cold.

Here god remembers god,
man remembers man
life and death hurry.

The Atlantic – winter of the world –
crows on the acropolis
hanging from oblivion.

Light and shadow.
The sealed sky advances
clutching its green thought.

Ice makes up soul and body
they feed on prophecy
beyond the borders of the realm.

*

The bitter bread of barbarians.
The violence of wind and cold
lashes your brain,
beats your soul. I don't see the world and yet it follows me like a shadow.
The grey of the sky threatens day and night enough to drive you mad.
Better not to look up; it creates vertigo, absence.
Plateaus, forests, crows all seem like assassins of my ancient bloodline
We live in lethargy, we think lethargically. For centuries.

Moss, lichens, green-blue-green on the branches of the bare birches,
in my youth, in Darsìa, during the dictatorship, I kissed them as if they
    were the bodies
of young women,
the spent gaze of borderland peoples, robbed of time,
they pass by indifferent. They walk like trunks.

From the West to the East, black clouds hold other rain, gusts of freezing
wind wound the arc of time. They hiss terribly
ocean's wild songs.
Torn branches on the streets of red earth, broken wings of night birds
hung in the air, lightning and thunder on the bay. The exhausted
    fishermen drink
their bitterness deep into the night inside the wet tavern.

Nightmares of the border
happy, well-paid slaves, court poets of the kingdom,
bringers of bloody war (heads of government, presidents of state) received
with every honor by those reigning. All the contorted streets of the world
    bring you to Empire.

My home in King Street is flooded by high tide. Oceanic night.
Water reaches my bed, it runs down my spine,
silently wets the sheets. Shivers.

Morning. Hope returns. The dark trains leave for the south: monsters
	kidnapped
from the mist. They run over the curved hills in a hurry, over the cold
	countryside
with its robins and blackbirds, they run like wild beasts ferocious after prey
filled with men, pets, purebred women.

On the dark greedy roofs they tear up their prey
white doves, bloody feathers.
I write after seven days of rain.

I feel the Mediterranean running in my veins
like alcohol. Mystery of the wound.

I remember.

*

Infinite rains falling through the years,
swallows flown away in the skies of the south.
Cups of wine that lovers drink
in cold country houses.

Fires from poppy plants flame up in the fields
from one season to the next, stars stolen from eternity.
Black birds with grey winter on their wings
return every December to the branches of the olive trees.

Laments heard through the villages, cities at war
bring winds; in your big eyes: tears,
nostalgia for your country. Purple clouds reflect sunset
onto the ripe breasts of maidens.

So many storms have passed through the valley,
the mountains and the sea, the sadness of exile.
Full moons illuminate the flowers of eros,
naked bodies sweaty with love.

*

Remaining without a home on the open water, naked prisons,
this is our destiny, the breaking of ice under our feet,
the trembling of Christmas roses only just opened
where can we hang the slender thread of infinite life.
And if we went back for good? he says, looking at the falcon
that drops from the high sky in a sharp dive,
panic among the blackbirds in the valley, the snow reflected
in the sharp eyes of the lynx waiting in ambush –
it can be any day, whatever date,
no regrets for these orphan places
not now now after. The call of the night bird
shakes the indigenous forest, pure and unmoving.
Expelled beyond the border we count the nights

www.ingramcontent.com/pod-product-compliance
Lightning Source LLC
Chambersburg PA
CBHW022009160426
43197CB00007B/351